TUSCANY

INSIDE THE LIGHT

WINTER

SPRING

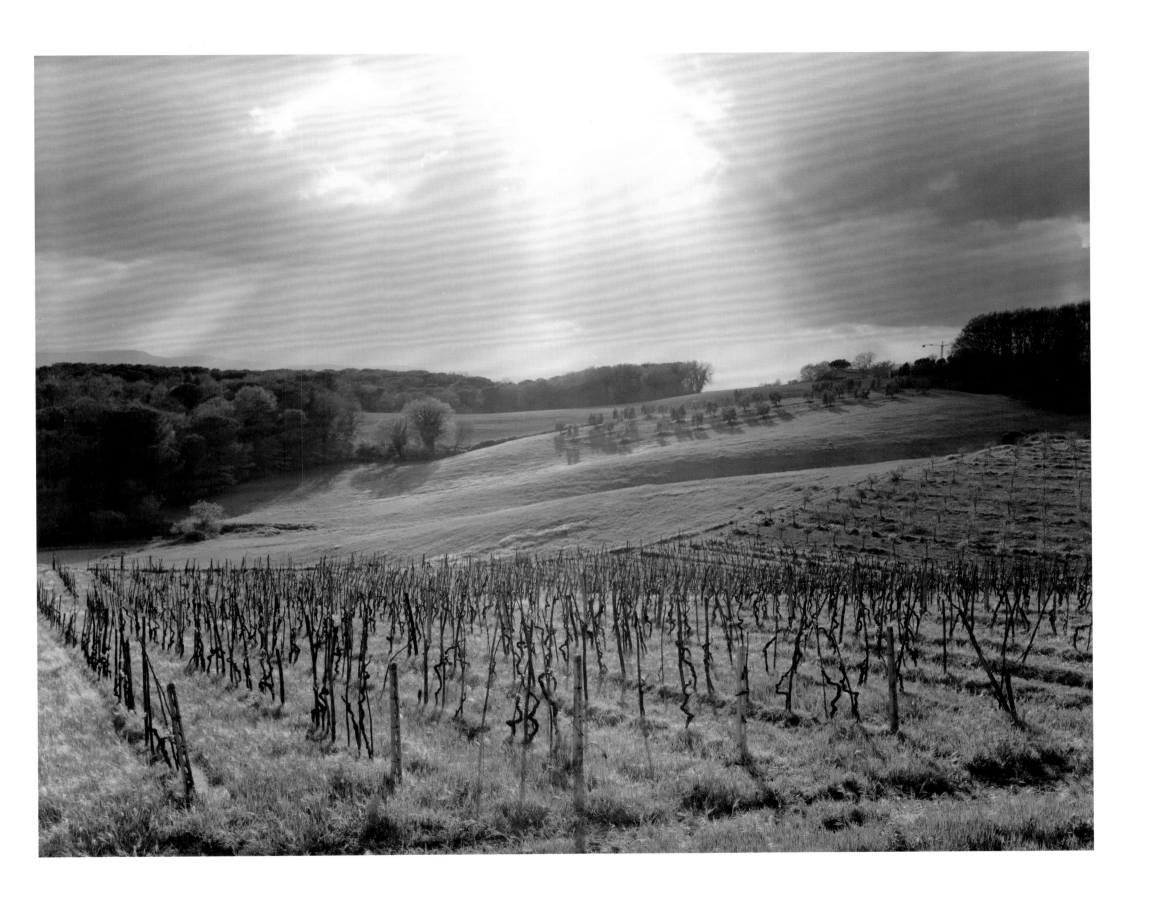

SUMMER

AUTUMN

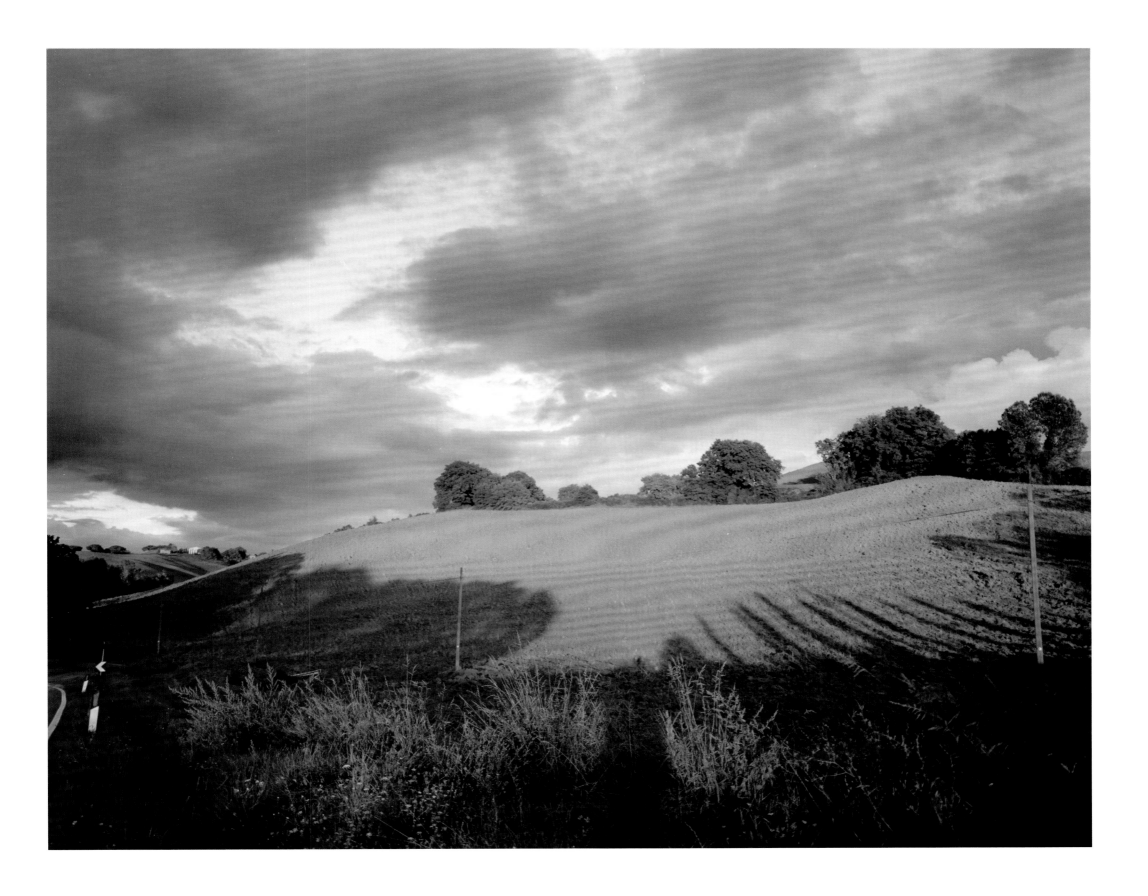

TUSCANY
INSIDE THE LIGHT

JOEL MEYEROWITZ

MAGGIE BARRETT

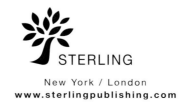

STERLING

New York / London
www.sterlingpublishing.com

For Gianni Mariotti

*W*e have been many places in this world where the light is remarkable. But having come to Tuscany for a decade, we understand that as spectacular as the light can be in other places, it is as a spectator that one usually experiences it. That is, the light is always over there, at a distance, and one stands back and marvels at it. But in Tuscany you are a participant, because the light is all-encompassing. Here, you are inside the light, and therefore connected to all that falls within its sphere: the land, the sky, the people. It is as though each of us has a designated ray of light that stitches us into the fabric of the universe. We experience a profound sense of belonging, not only to each other, but to history, to the moment, and to the possibility of a brighter future. And so we invite you to journey with us through the seasons, in the hope that each of you will find your place inside the light.

WINTER

So this is it…the pure winter light, pulsing outside the dense fog as though all the stars that ever were and ever will be have joined forces, pixilating the air with a mist of pulverized diamonds.

PLATE I

PLATE 2

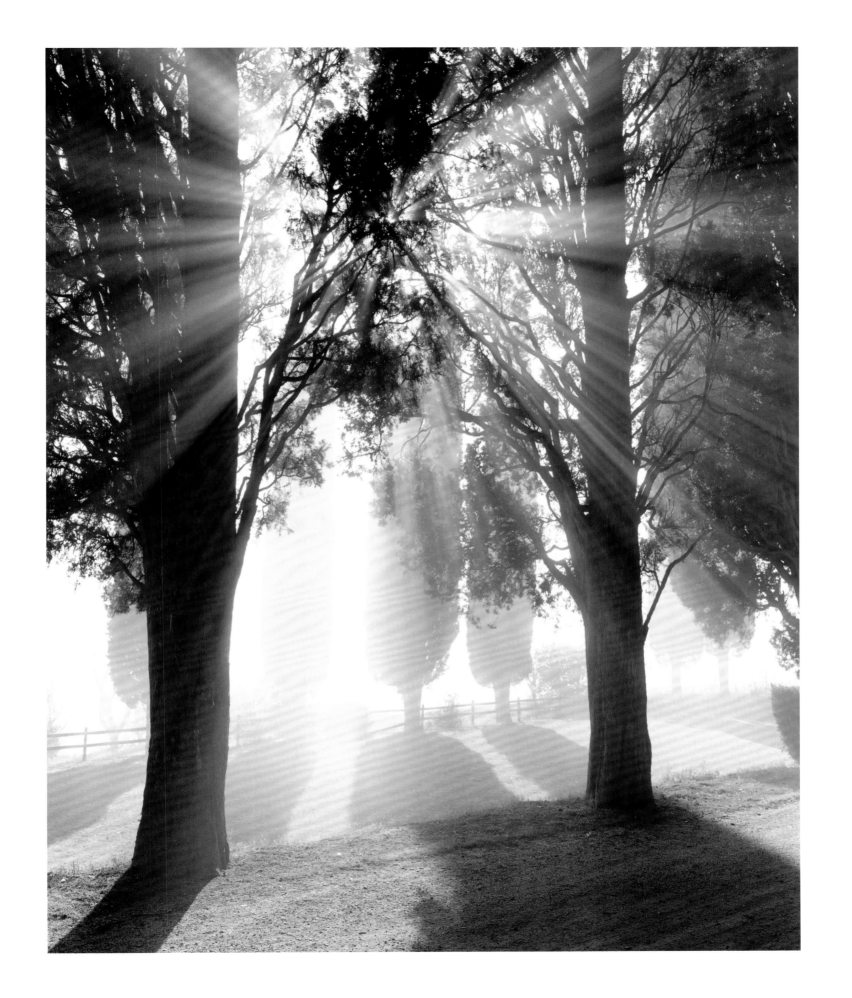

Plate 3

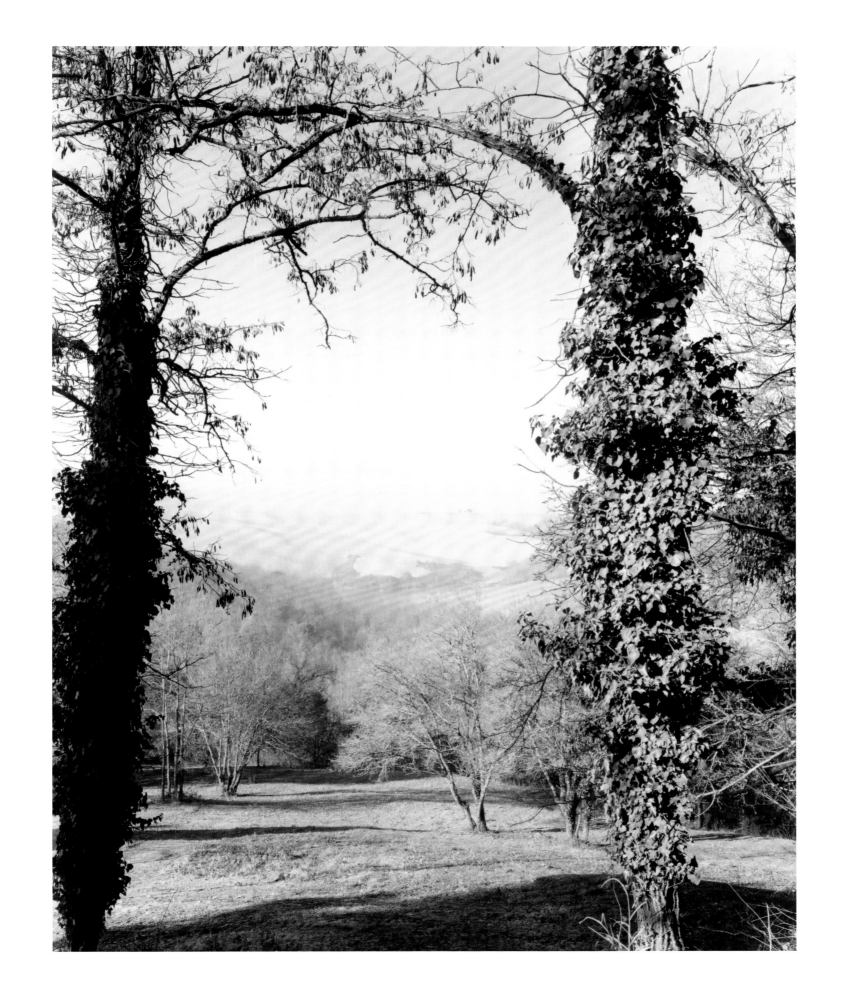

*C*urvaceous hills recline like a never-ending nude lazing in the sunlight. Barren of any seed or outcrop, the hills become pure form, color, and texture. And, oh, what color! At first glance a sandy gold that seems to graze the retina, and once grazed the pupil looks anew and sees sage and mustard and ochre and, up there in a fold near the sky, a lick of lavender. The earth's crumbly texture, made from plowed earth, rain, and perhaps a sprinkling of *olio*, resembles a coarse, hearty polenta. And so this undulating terrain of texture and color pits itself against the opaque blue of the sky, and you long to take a bite. What makes this so immensely satisfying, this marriage of opposites, the one so rough, the other smooth? Sky and earth, each remarkable on its own, when layered one atop the other create a profound union, the likes of which we mortals dream.

PLATE 4

PLATE 5

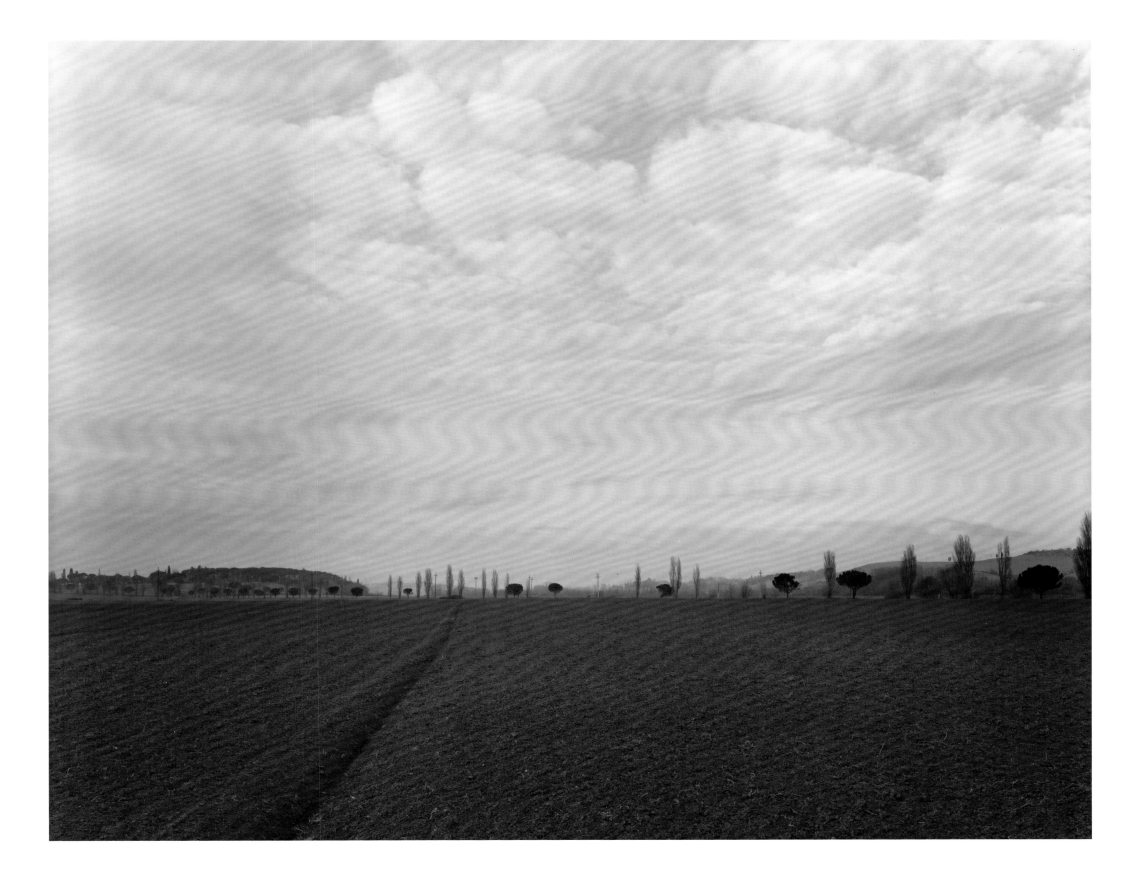

PLATE 6

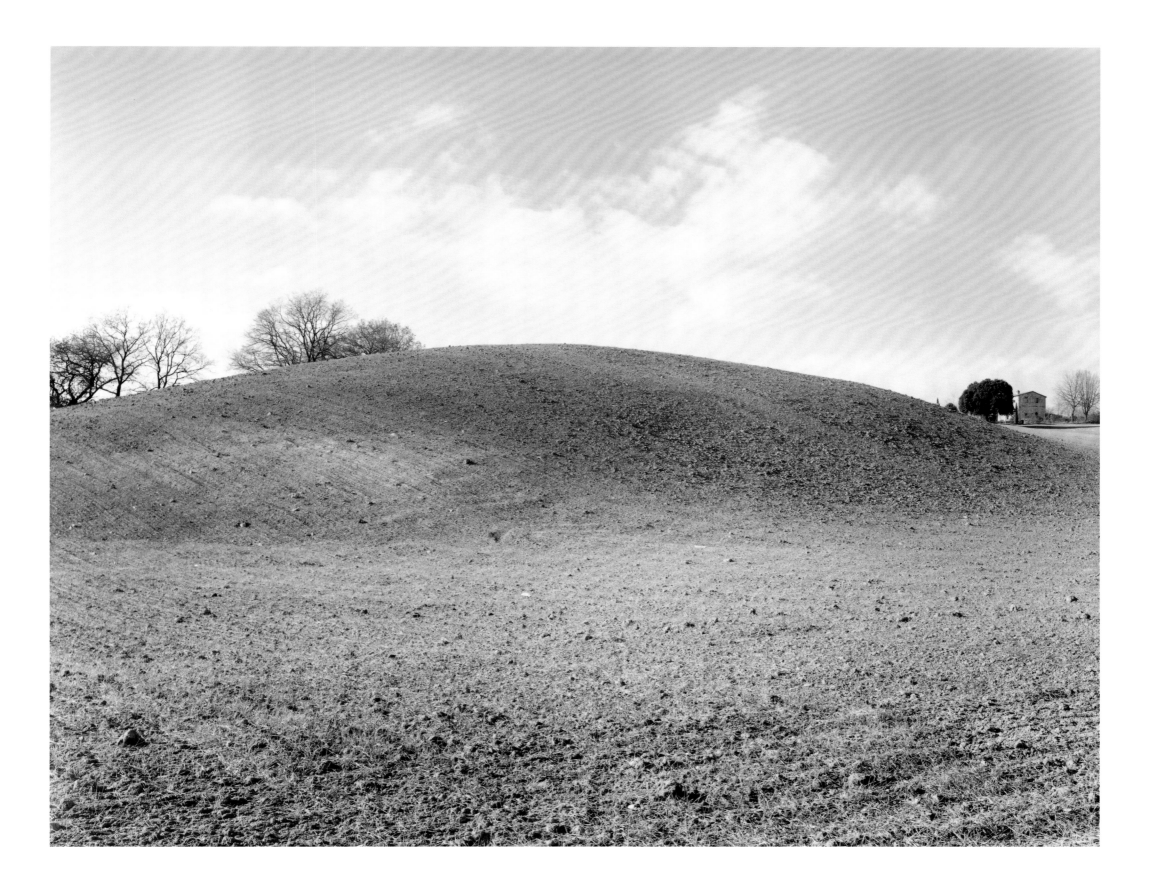

A tufted line of trees crosses the horizon: above, the milky blue sky; below, rolling down the slope, a field of threadbare carpet. Centuries of sowing and growing and harvesting have worn the earth down like a well-trod stair runner, reminding us that that which has been eroded by time has also become its essential self.

PLATE 7

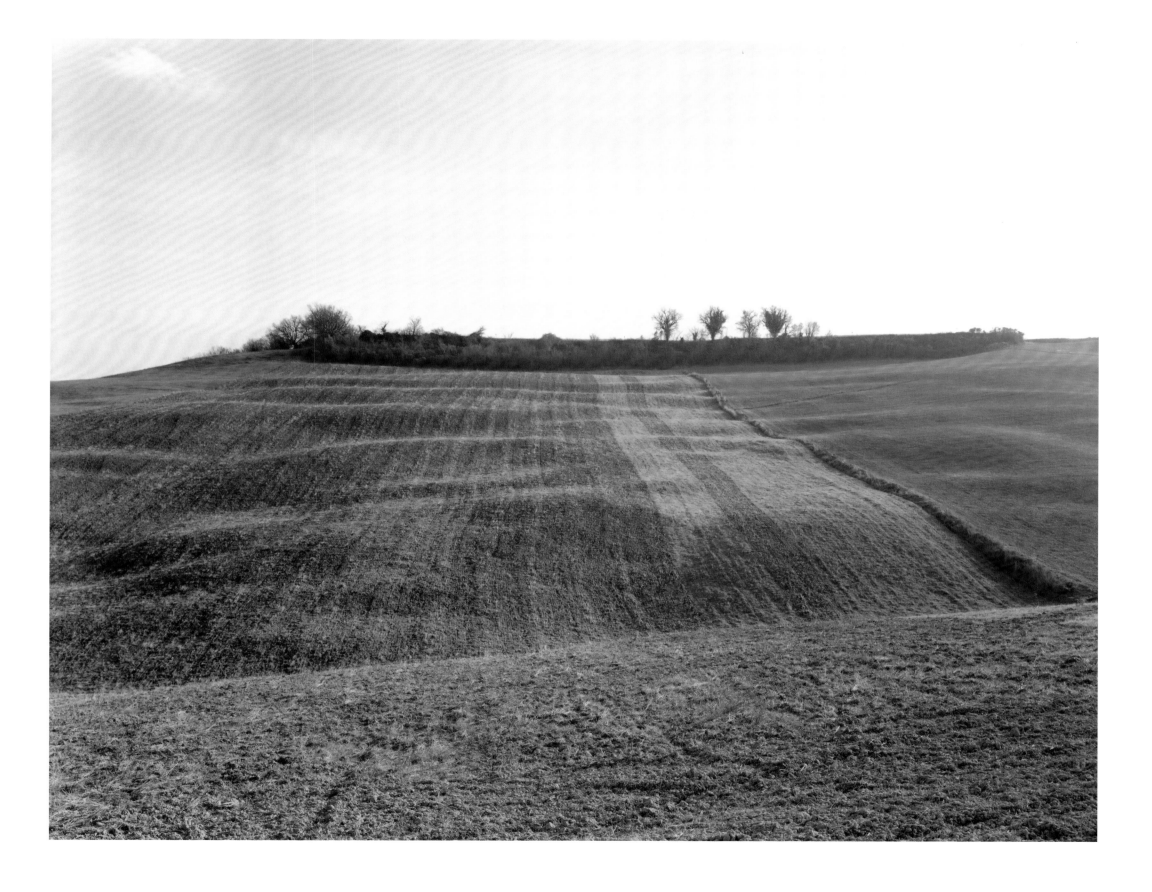

*T*oday the frost is so dense it looks like a light fall of snow. Down in the valley a gleaner, bent in the morning sun, picks and peels the last of the dried corn. A tractor scrapes its blades through the frozen earth, a sound that puts us in mind of summer. Clumps of frozen, muddy sod—turned over back in the autumn—sit now like truffles dusted with confectioner's sugar, while between the clumps the winter grass tinkles with icy light. We wait in the car in our down jackets and, in spite of everything that tells us it is winter, feel the sun as warm and gentle as a June morning. Time and light are inextricably linked here, so that each season holds within it the other three, as though the light gathers time and gives it back to us in its totality.

PLATE 8

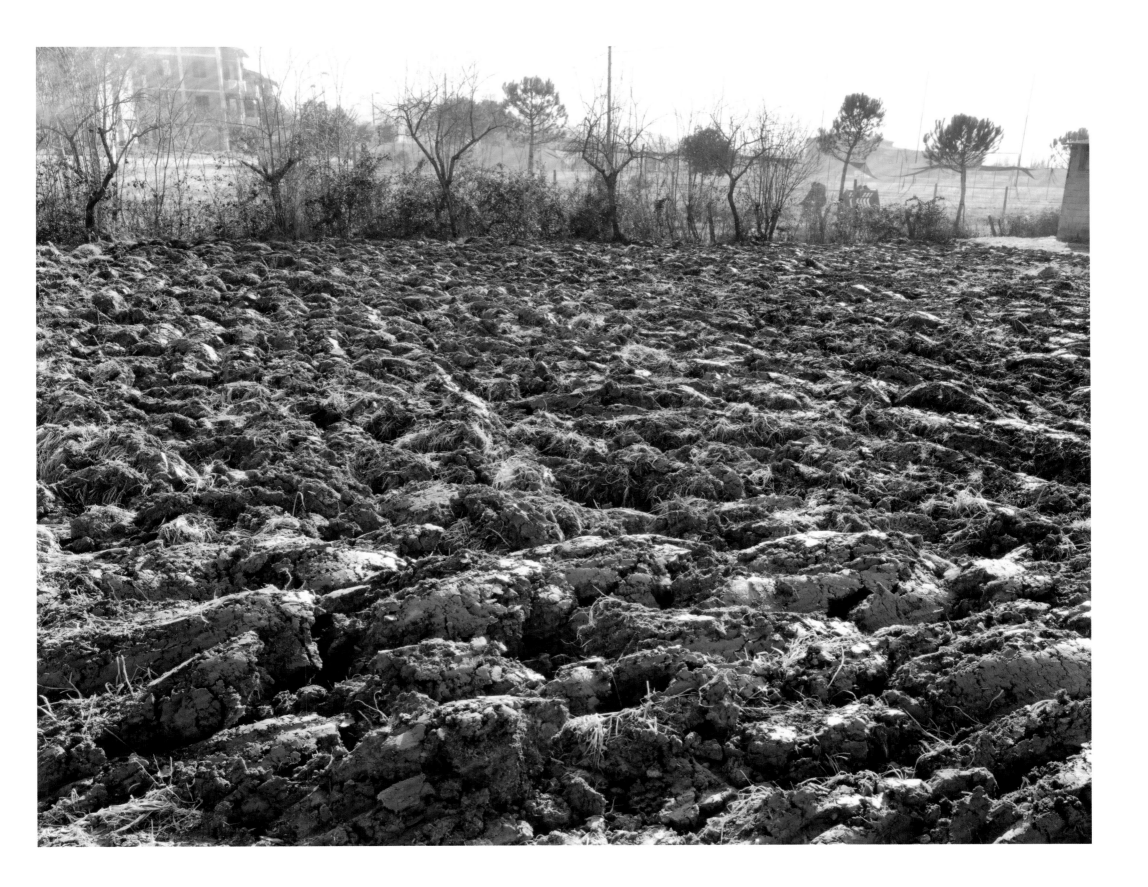

PLATE 9

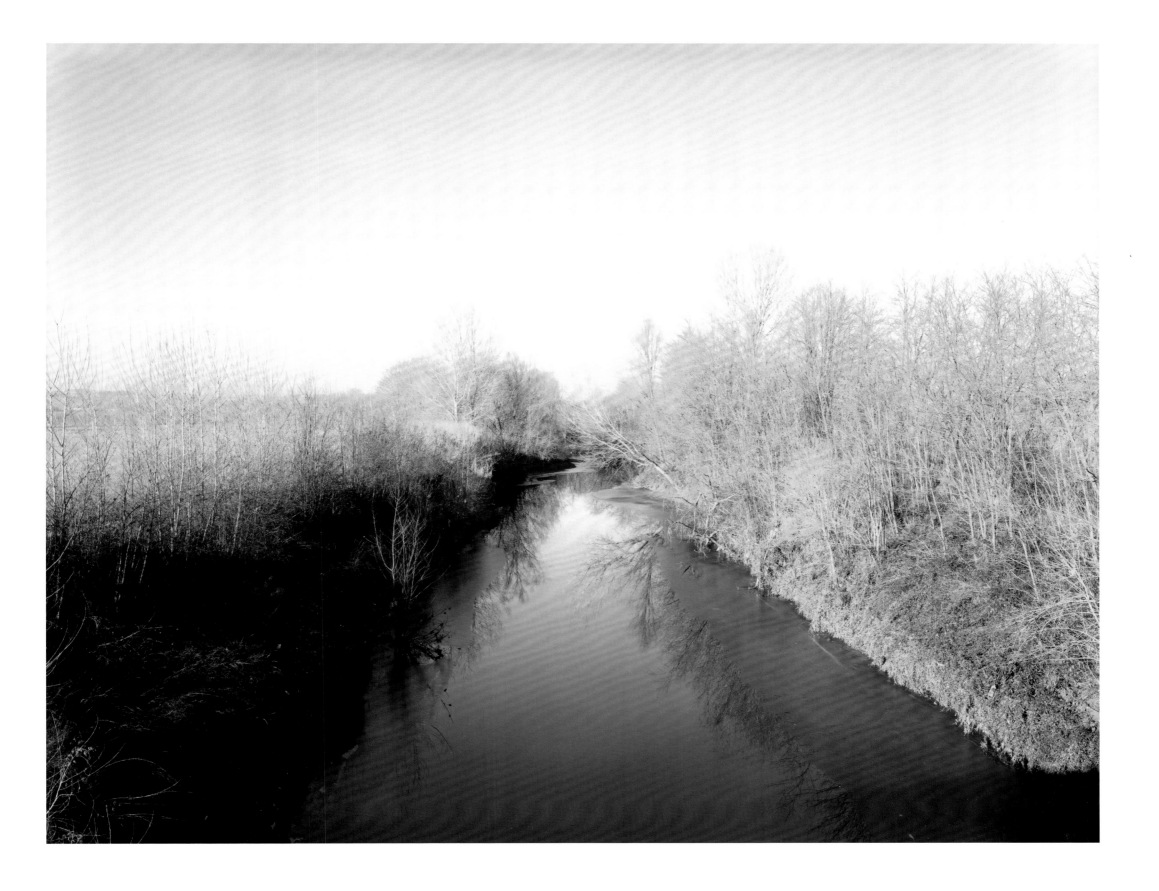

Plate 10

Overleaf: Plates 11 and 12

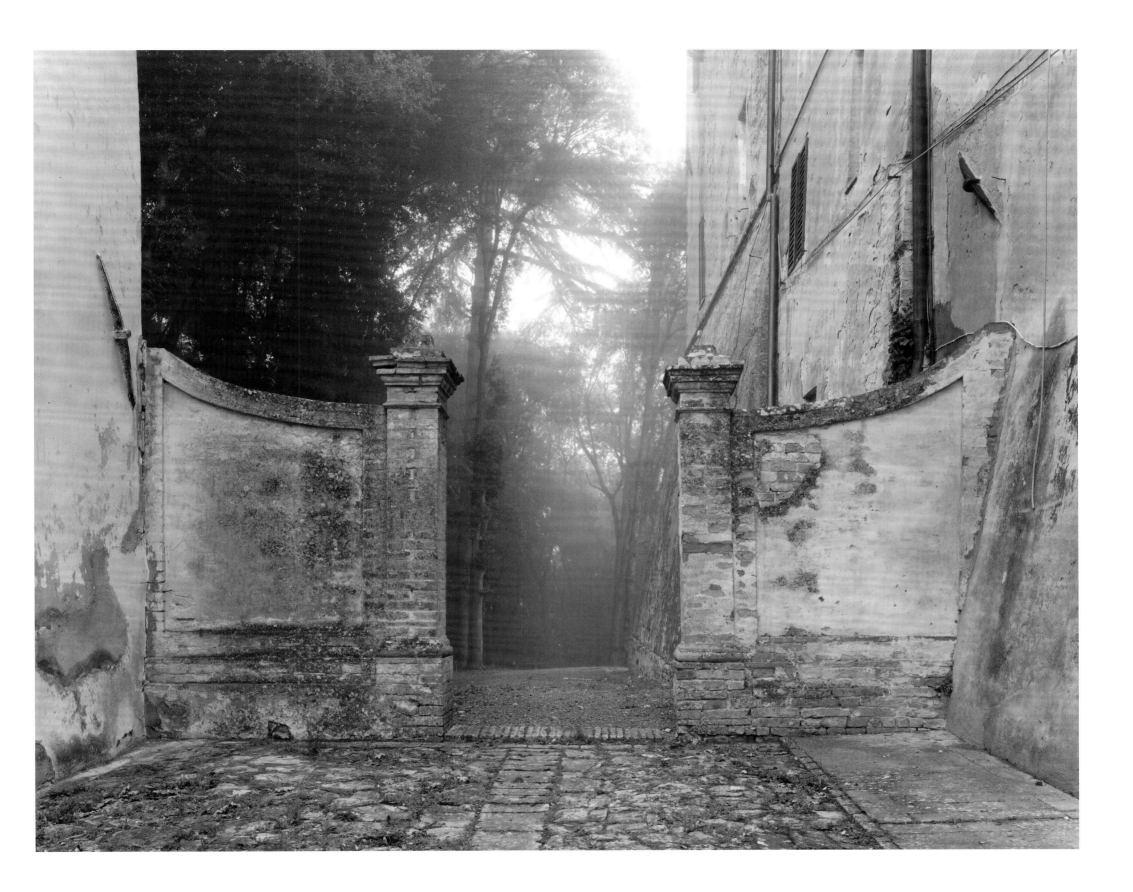

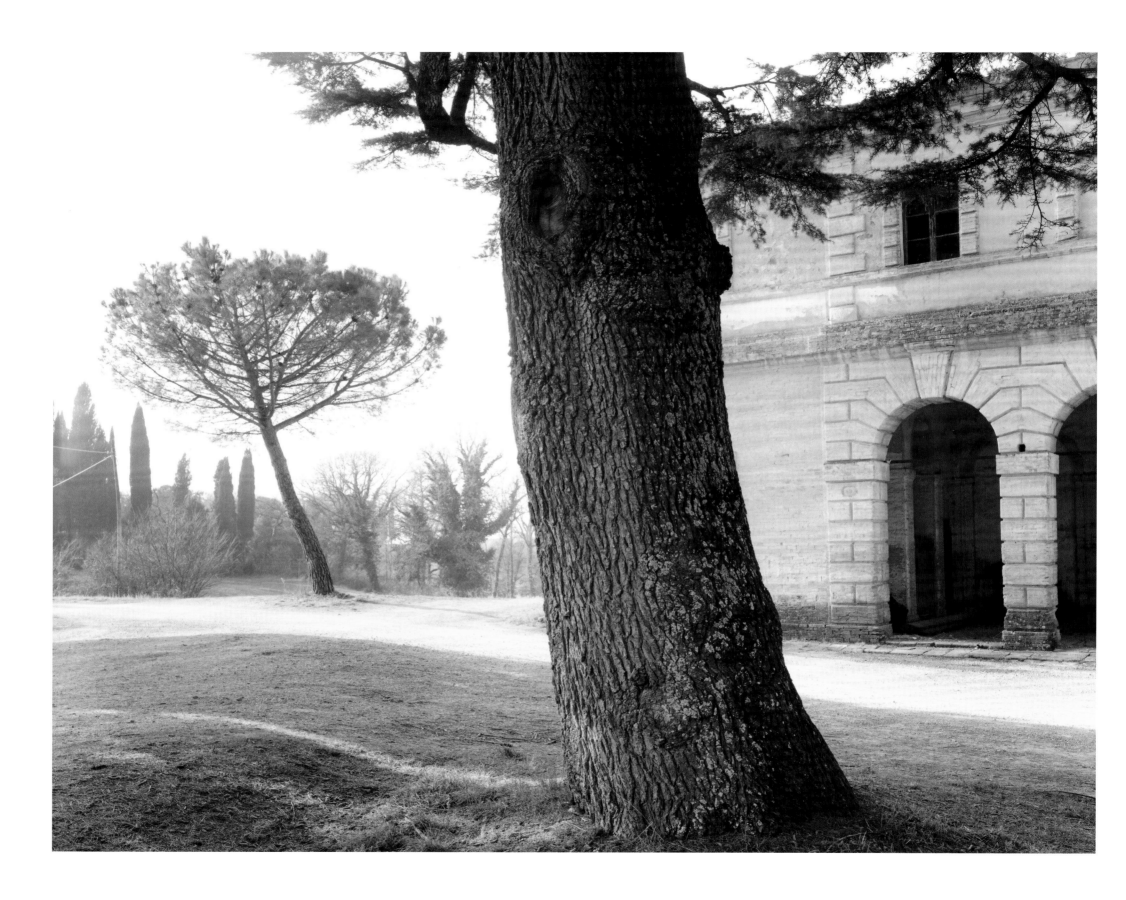

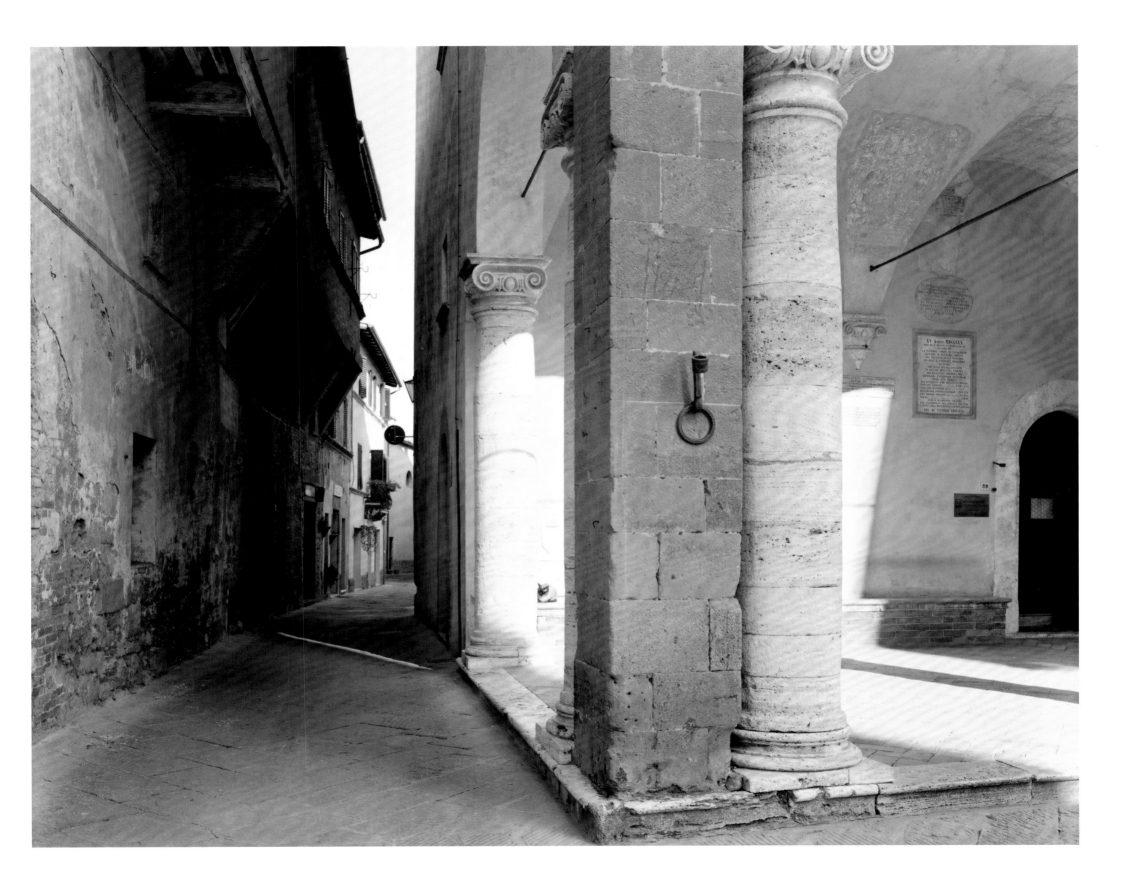

$\mathcal{I}$ am mesmerized by a wall of succulent ivy, and

wonder why this seemingly mundane piece of nature captures my attention. The longer I look, the

more I see it as a recipe for successful living. Just a few weeks ago there was not a leaf to be seen

on this wall. Back then, it appeared a skein of dead vines, barren, tattered, clinging to the stone from

centuries of habit. But of course, it was not dead, merely dormant. This is the simple lesson that

nature reveals to me this morning: the rebirth we so desperately long for cannot be gained solely

by searching and inventing and consuming. To grow, we must also be prepared to lie dormant.

PLATE 13

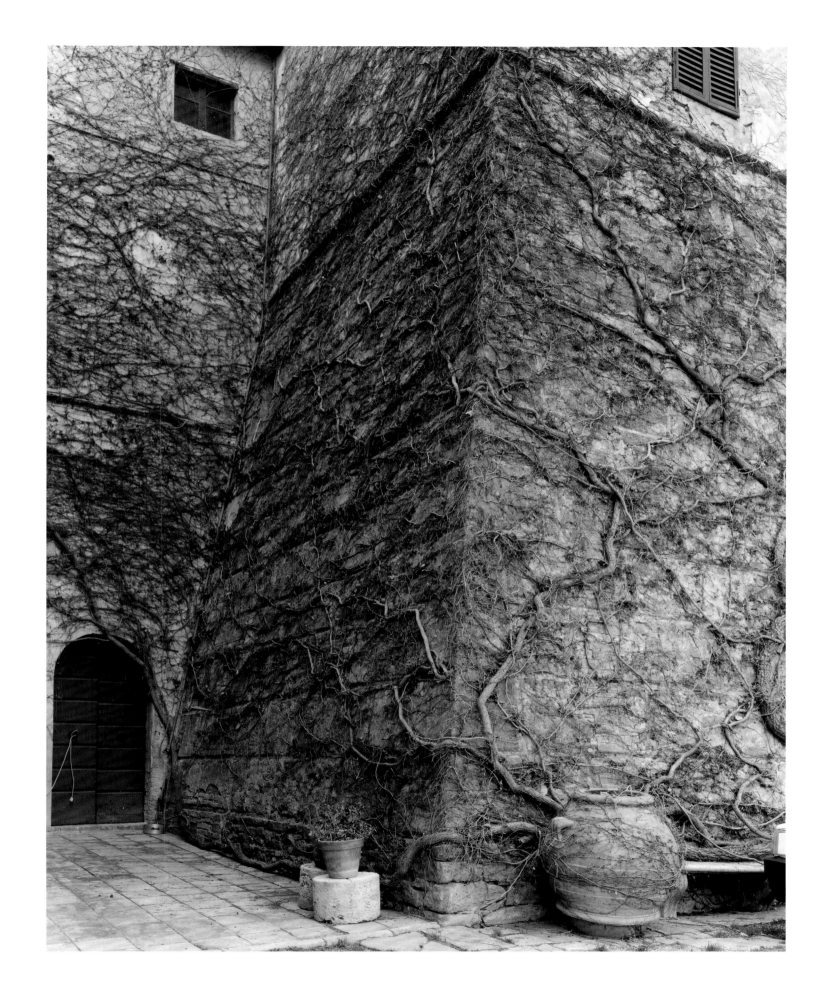

PLATE 14

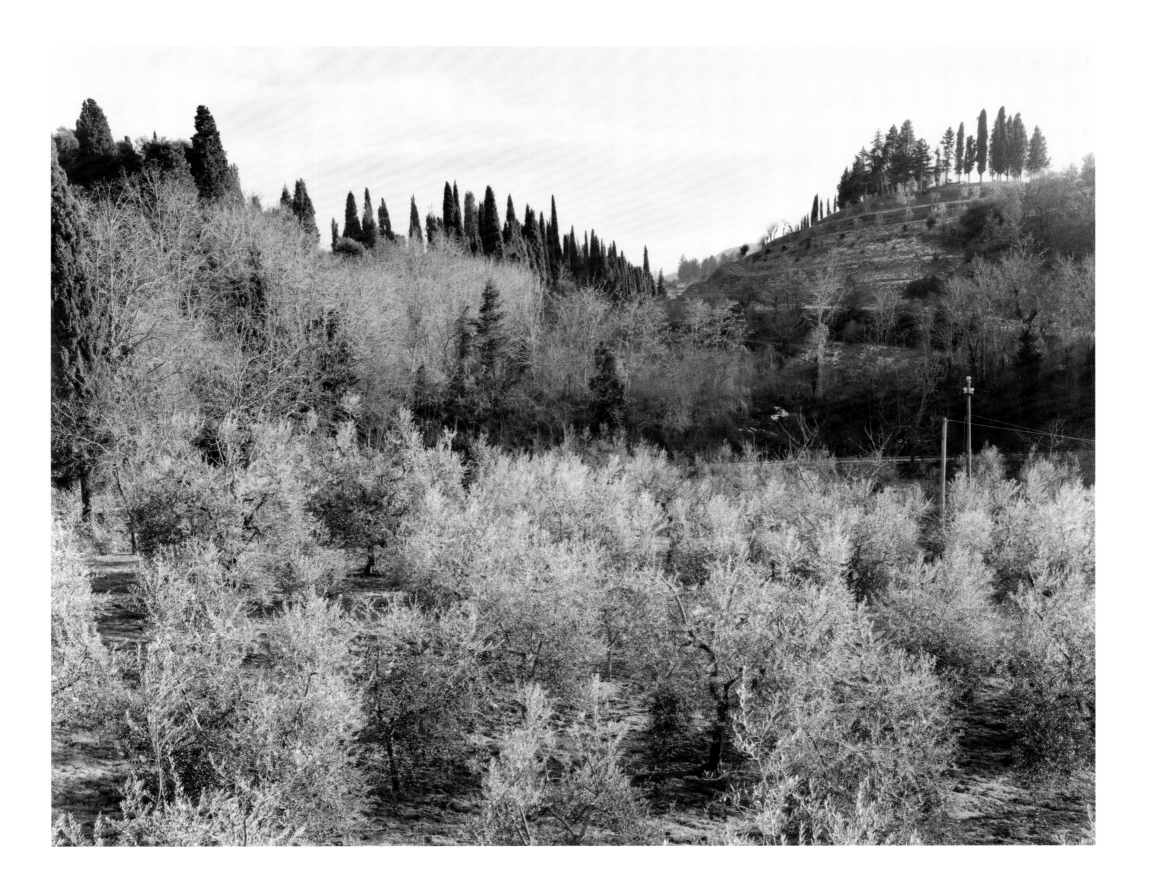

PLATE 15

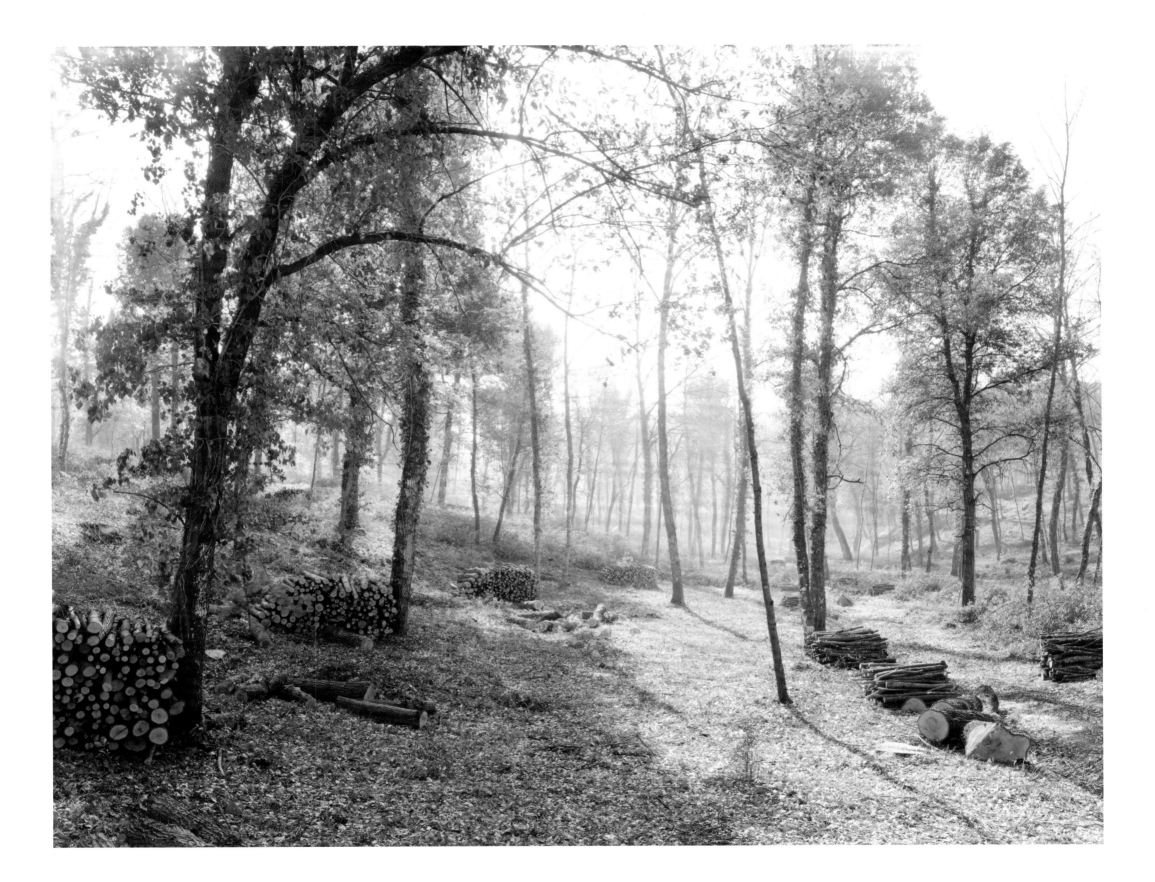

*I*nside the old guardhouse the light filters in from one small window and scatters through the dust motes before coming to rest on a spread of ruby meat glistening on the table. The tap, tap, tap of exquisitely sharp knives accompanies the spare movements of three men butchering wild boar. The flesh appears lit from within, as though the creatures' spirits still inhabited their separate piles of suet and ribs, loin and liver, trotters and chops. There is nothing tragic here. Sides of meat hang like violins seasoning in the still, cold air. There is something almost holy about this ritual. Maybe it is the knowledge that the pigs led a good life here in the woods, well fed, chomping and romping in the mud for four seasons, and now their time has come.

PLATE 16

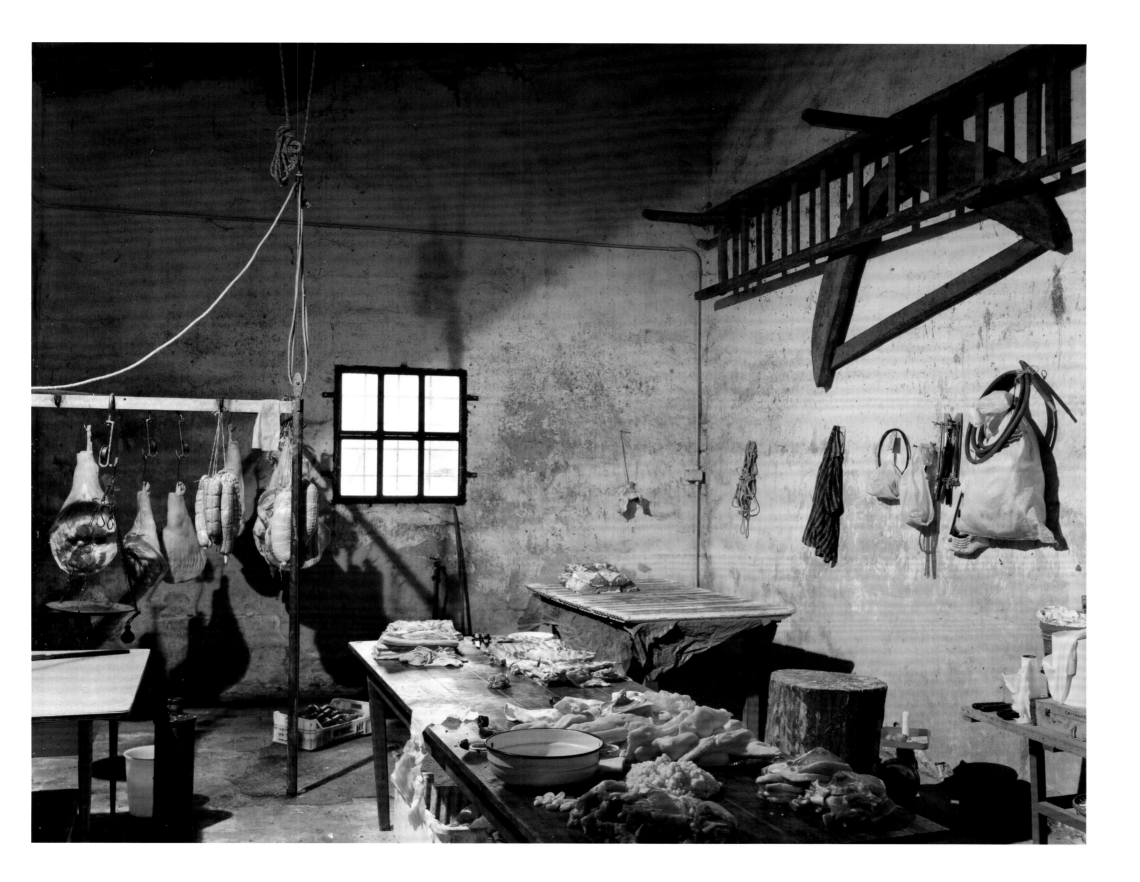

PLATE 17

OVERLEAF: PLATES 18 AND 19

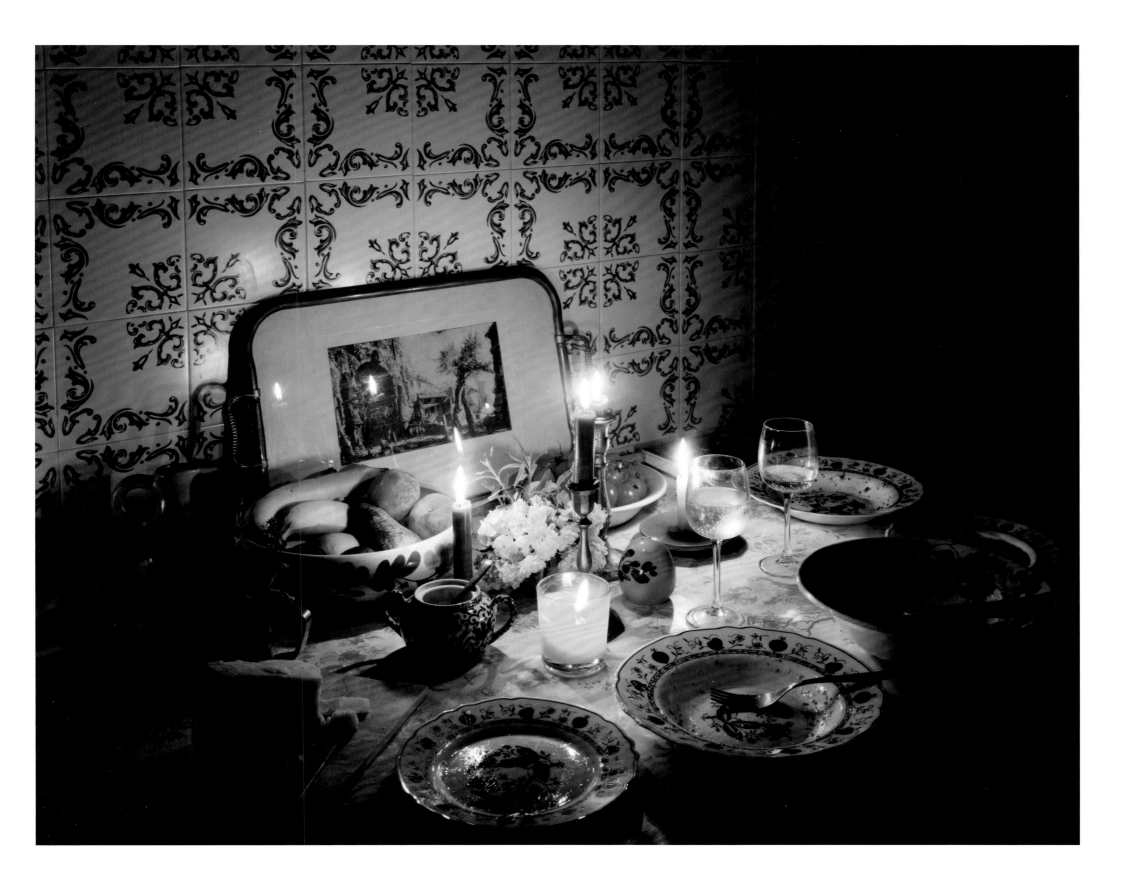

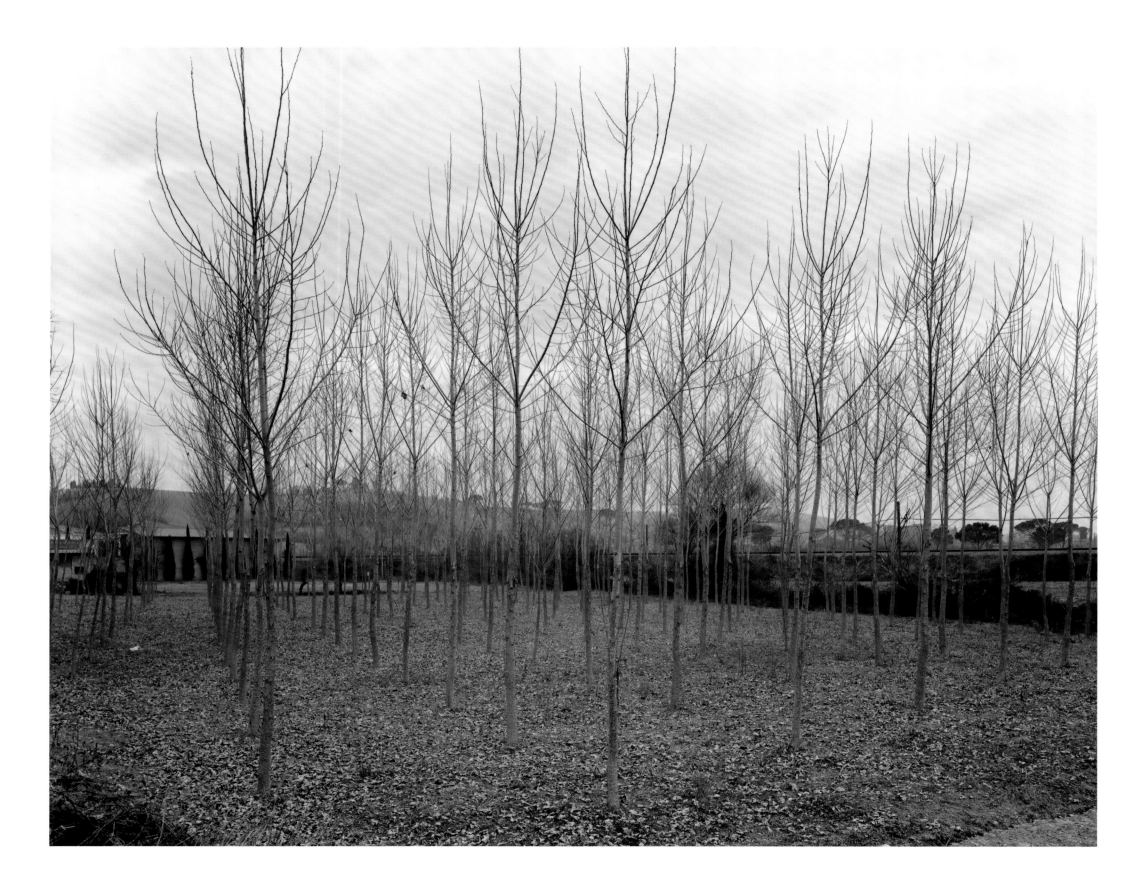

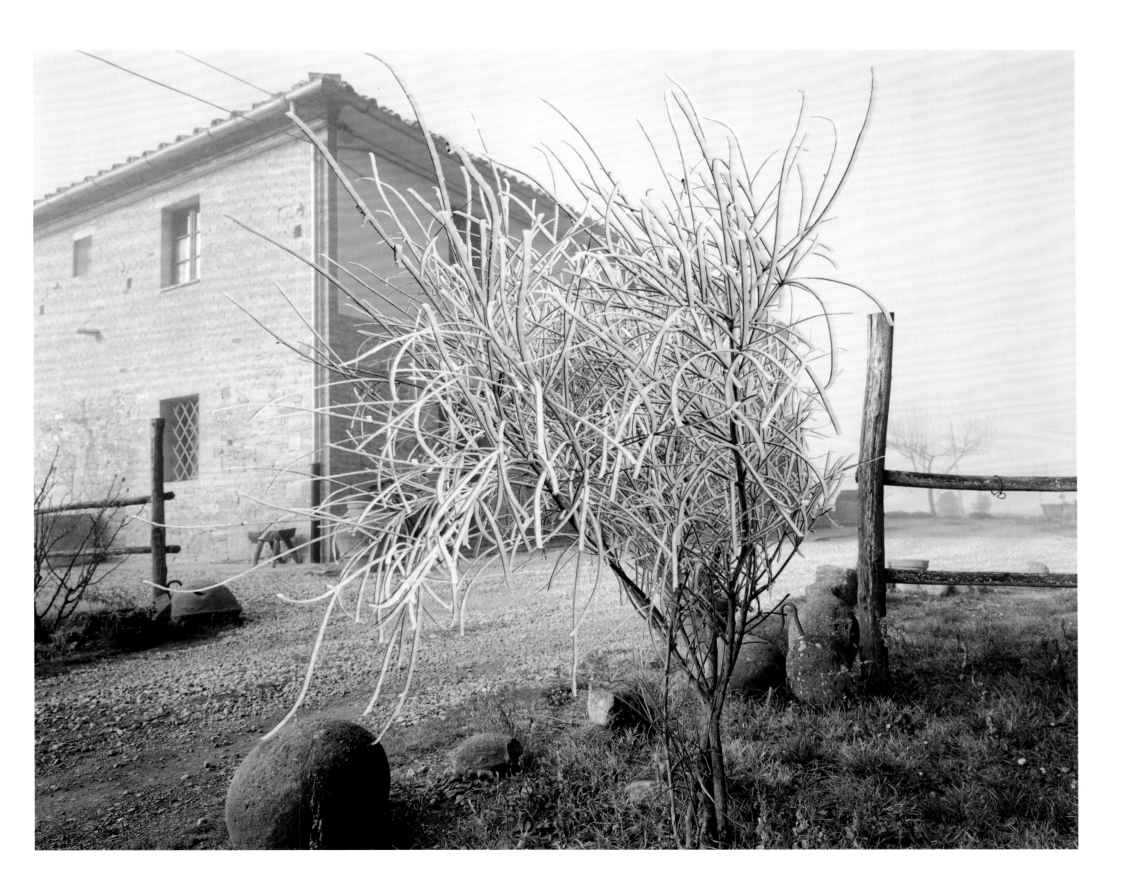

PLATE 20

PLATE 21

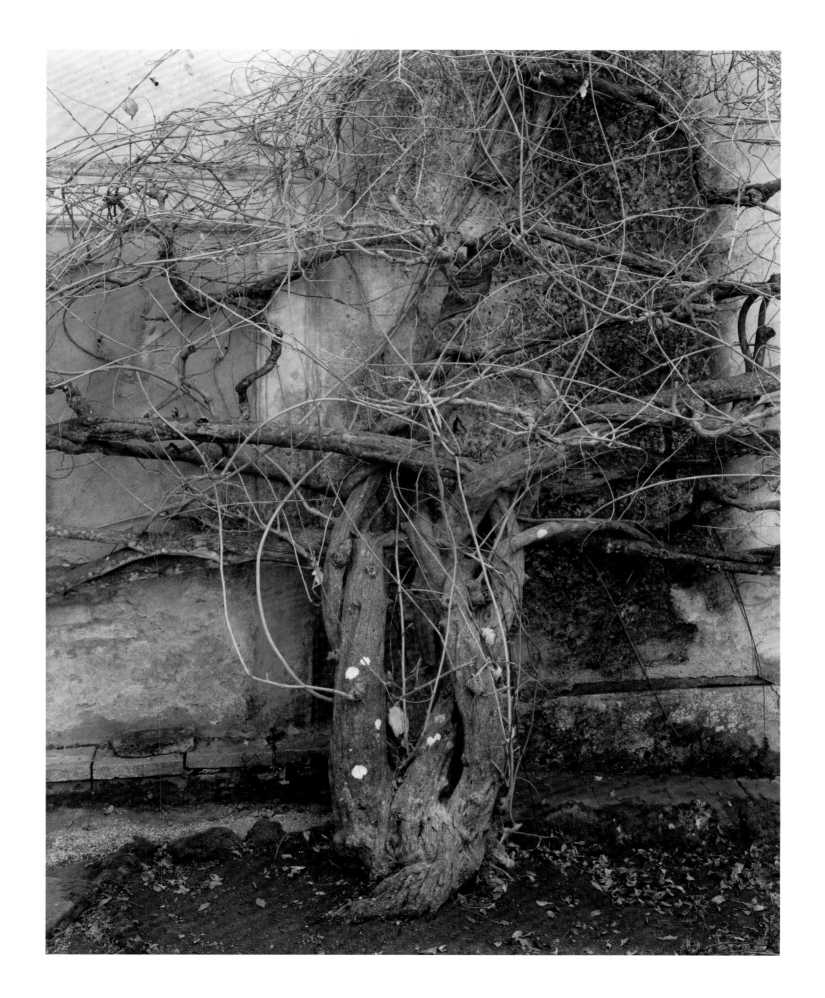

S P R I N G

*T*he wisteria is raining from its sooty vines, a drape
of mauve lament. Pendulous, faded even as it arrives, yet still a gasp against the pale, sandy stucco.
As wistful as its name, this exquisite blossom that comes at the beginning of spring appears old
before its time, emblematic of life in its grapelike formation, yet funereal in shade and scent.
Wisteria. The Queen of Ambiguity.

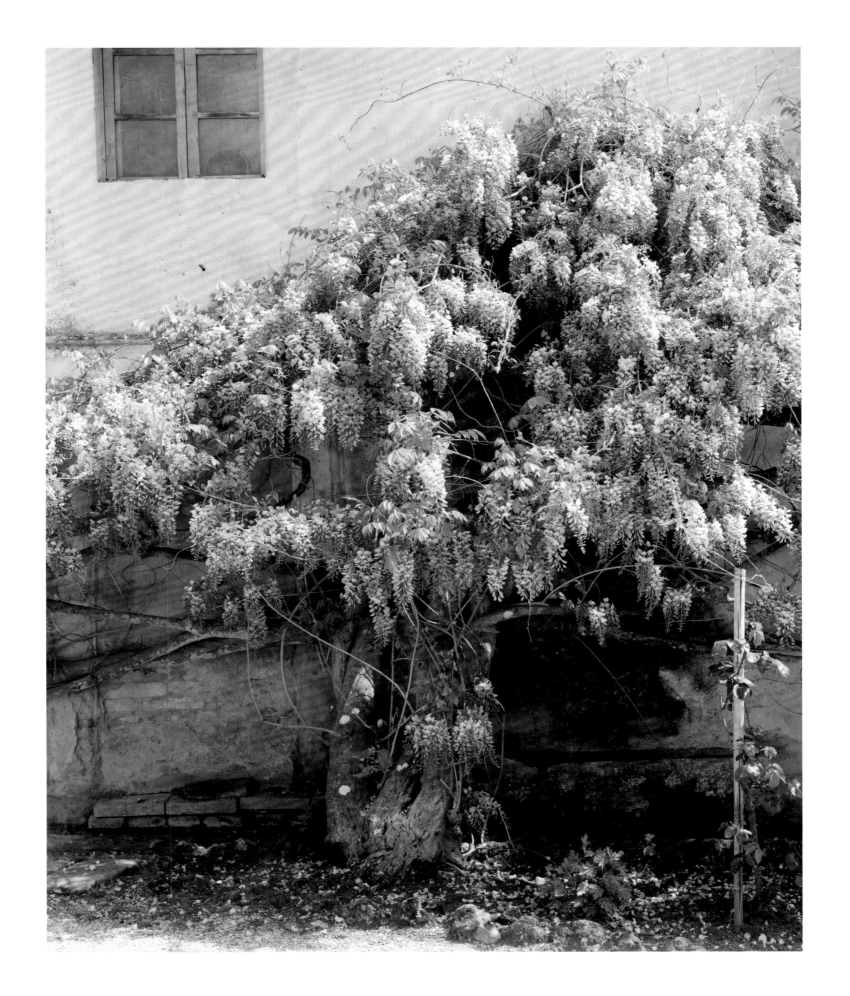

PLATE 23

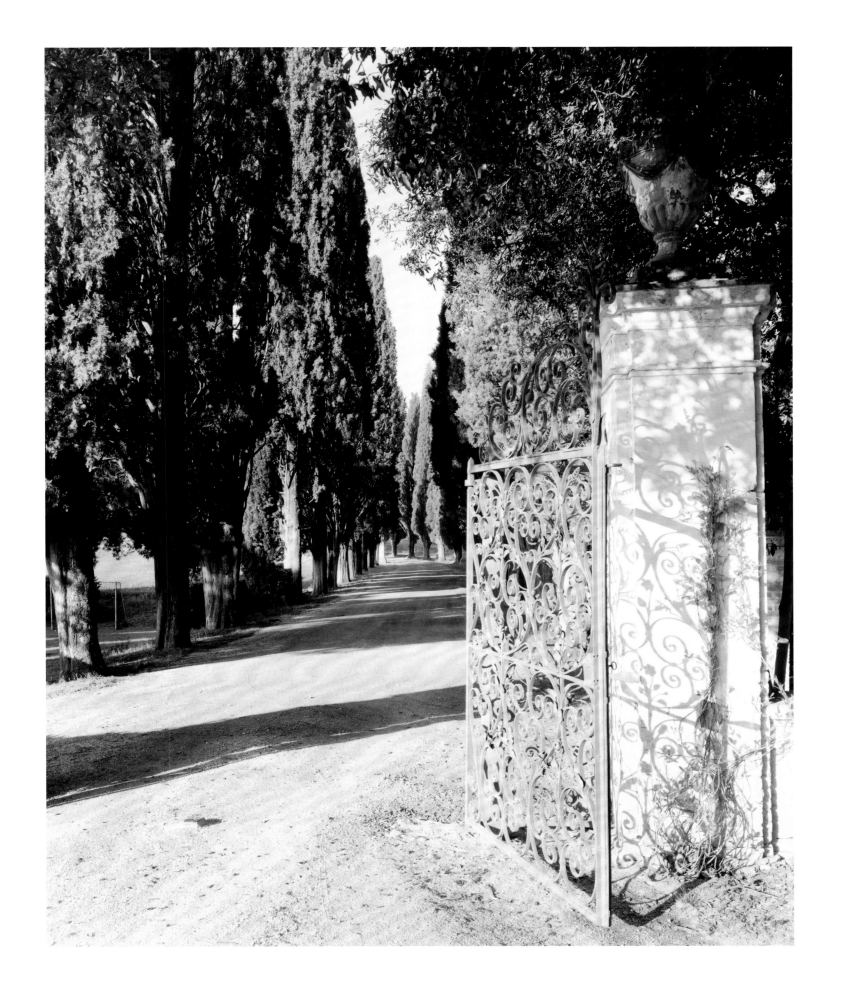

Plate 24

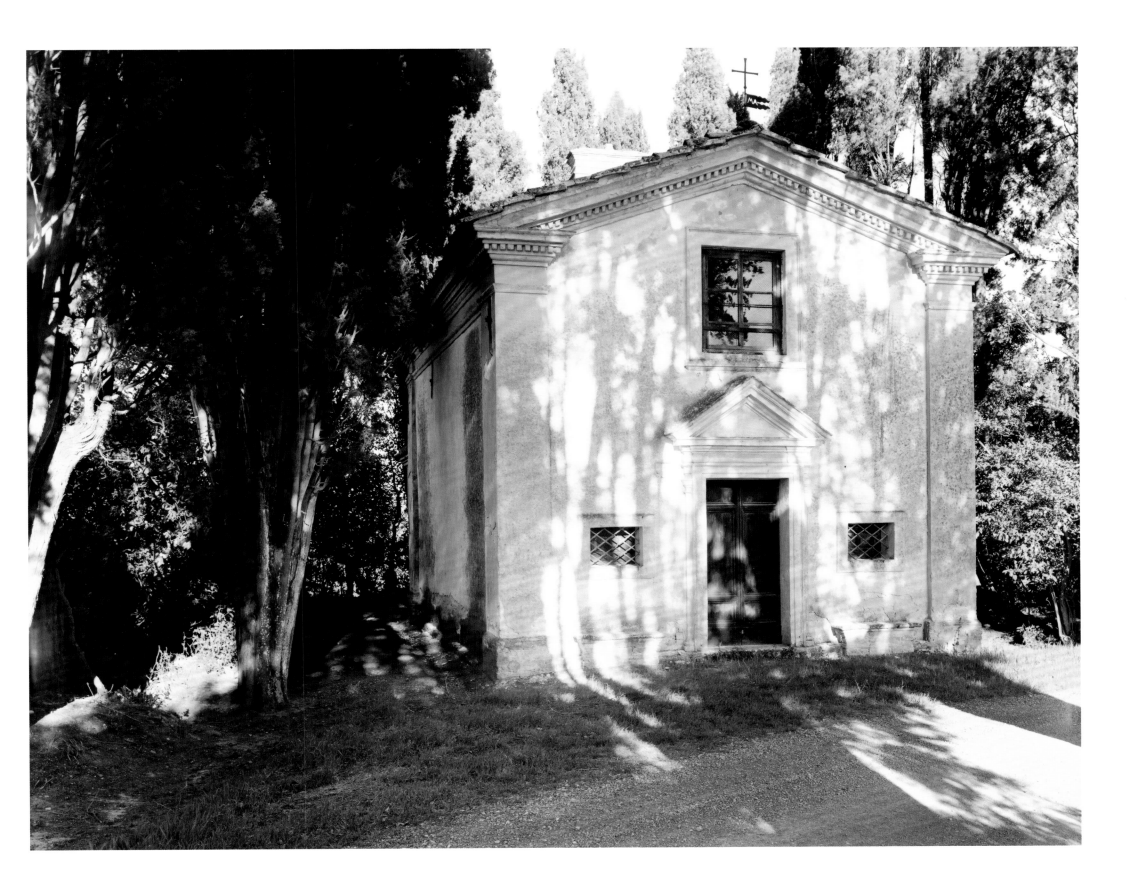

*M*y husband says it's the day the air turned green, and so it is. A vibrant buzz of chartreuse sings out from every branch, while the green of the young wheat fields has the same urgent tone as blood, the same thrill, danger even, as if to say every birth carries its imminent death.

We look down and across a small valley formed by a slope of tilled earth on the left and an equally sloping vineyard on the right. The one is mouth-wateringly empty, the other a dance of charcoal stumps whose outstretched arms reach for each other as they jig across a fuzz of grass. It is mad here. Wild wood doves coo nonstop in a nearby copse, and even though the air is still, even though the landscape appears not to move, the impression of latent energy is enough to make one strip off one's clothes, leap across the berry canes, and cavort with bacchanalian abandon, down there, down in the beginning of time.

PLATE 25

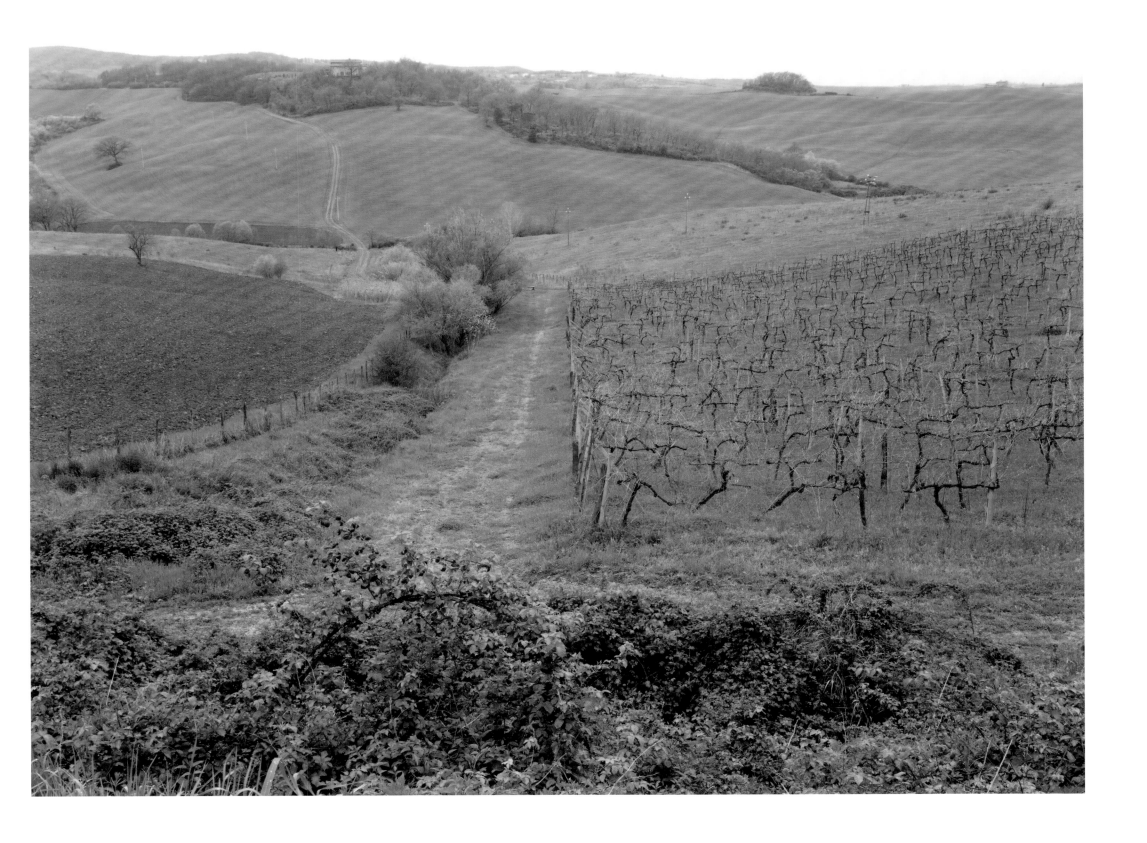

PLATE 26

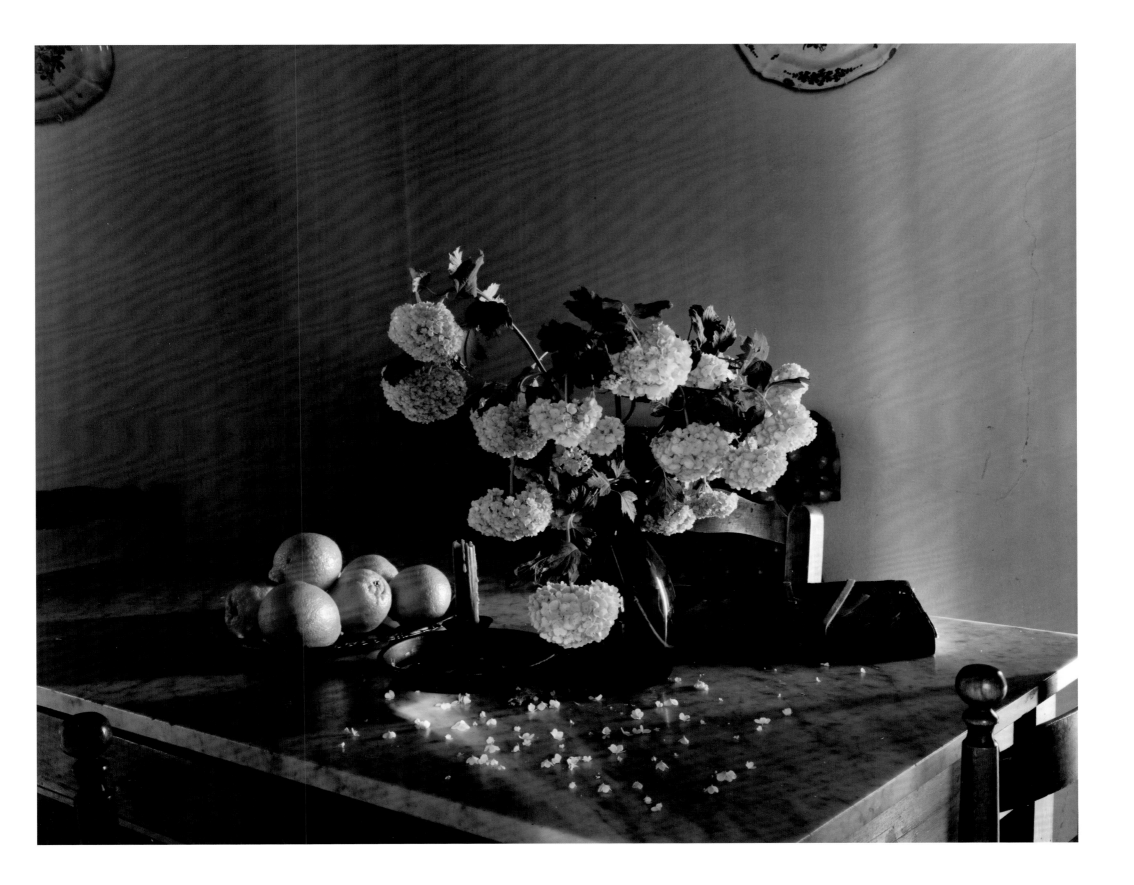

If only religion were this simple. To come to a place like this and be bathed in its soft, rosy light. What a baptism. No preaching, no superstition, no punishment. Light and silence. Only listen, and perhaps a prayer will come to your lips. Seventeen crosses, and on the eighteenth a whisper of Jesus, showing us the delicacy of surrender, at one with the instrument of his death.

PLATE 27

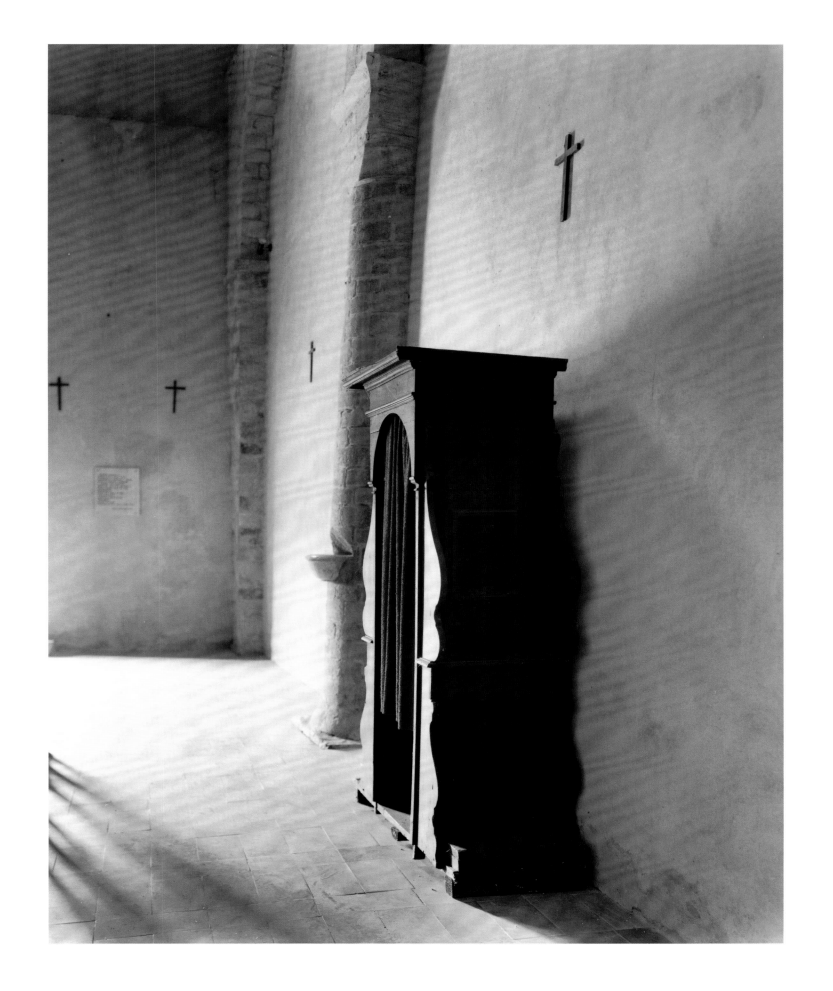

PLATE 28

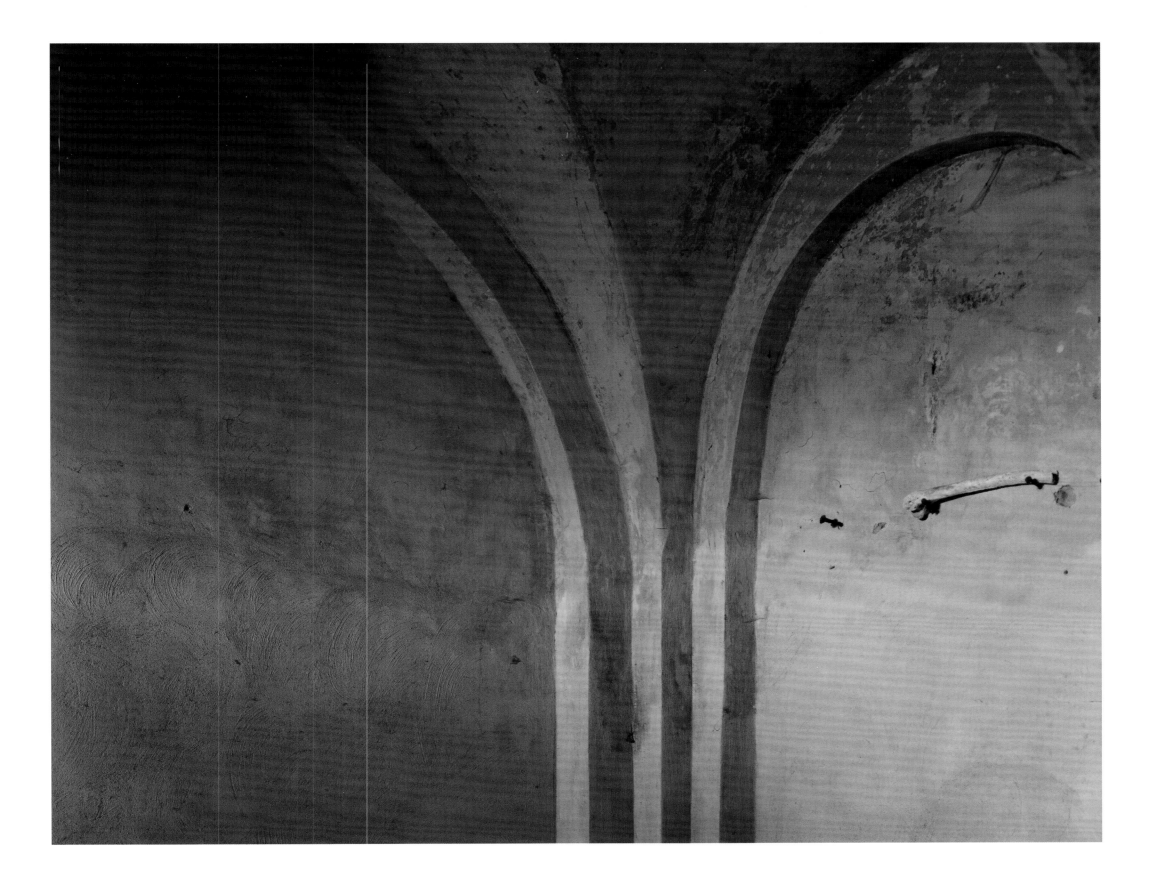

Space, time, light. Add to these worldly gifts the human

gifts of labor, vision, and sensibility and you might just get a fireplace that is both cathedral and

cave, temple and heart. I would wish to have sat before this one when the first flames rose,

can imagine hands reaching toward the heat, the gigantic shadows leaping out from the hearth

and dancing over faces and walls, ceiling and floor. You can almost hear the mighty roar and crackle

of the wood—whole trunks burning, the smoke rising inside the ivory skin of the chimneybreast.

To sit in this immense room is to lament all that we have abandoned in the name of progress.

PLATE 29

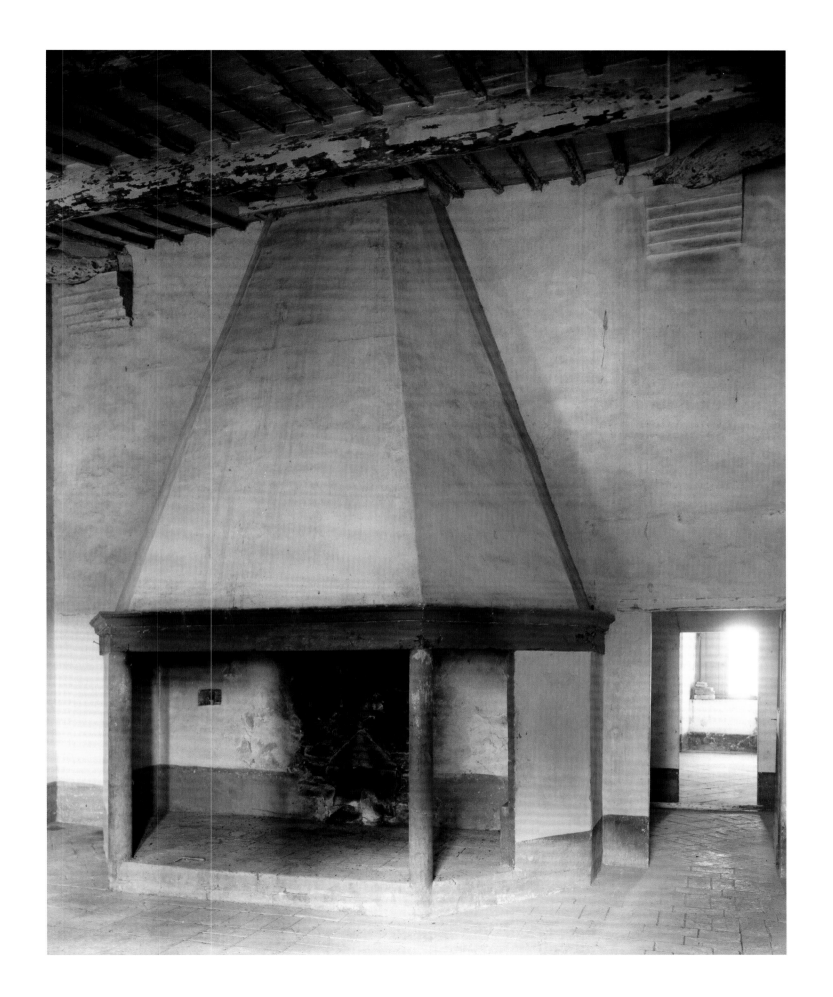

PLATE 30

OVERLEAF: PLATES 31 AND 32

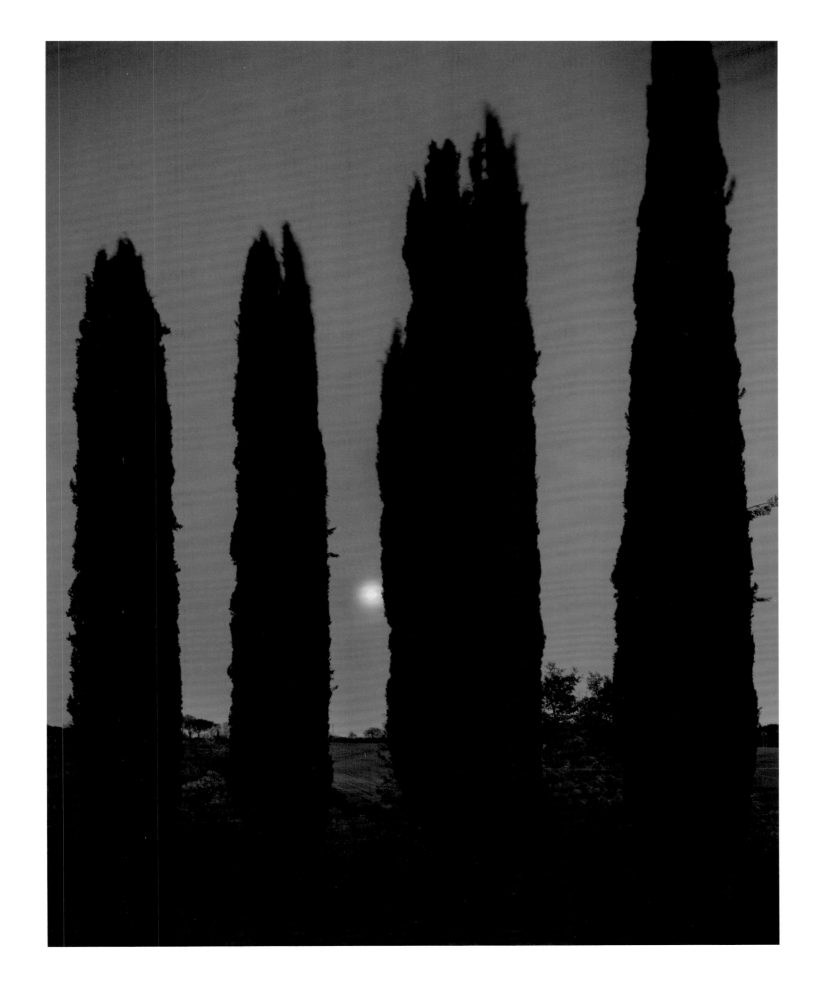

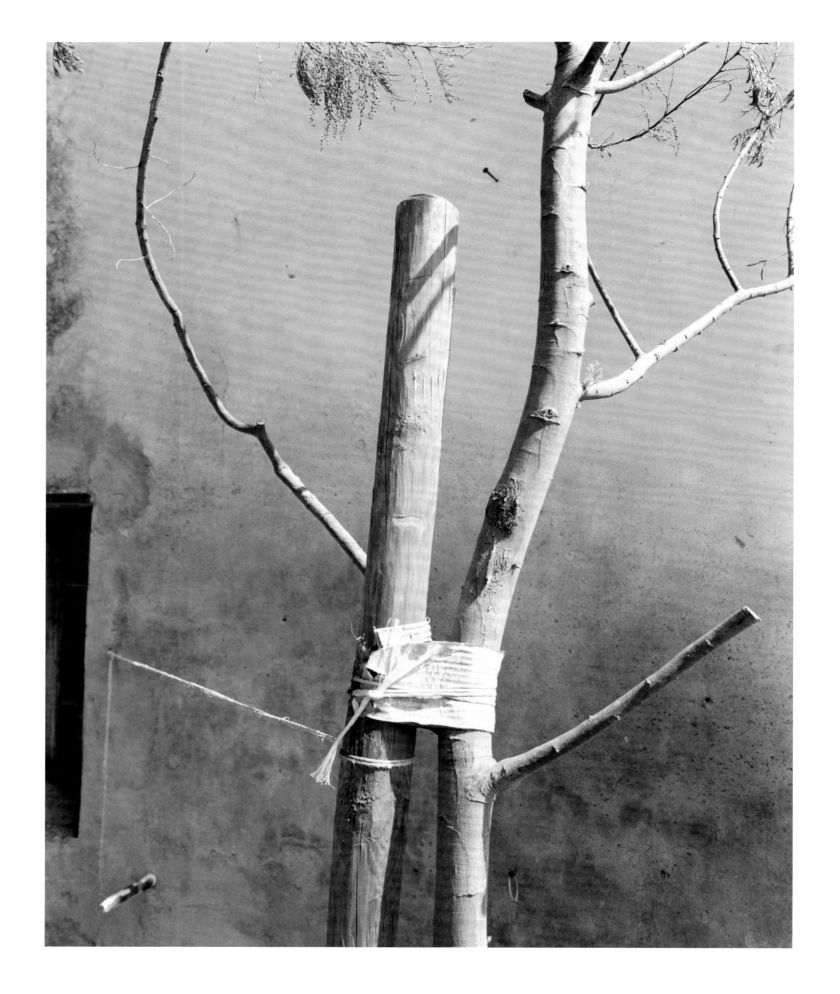

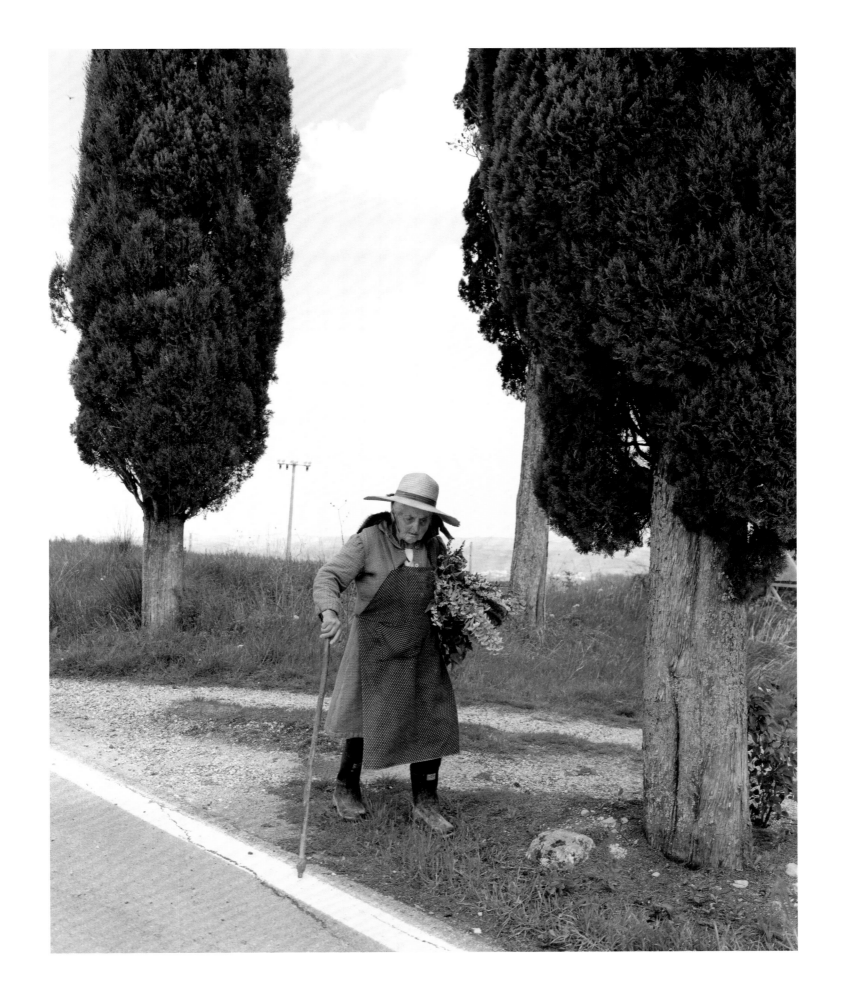

*W*hat is it that strives in us to become new? To blossom and reach for the heavens before falling, falling to the earth? That tree, how many winters has it died to, and then, in the space between seasons, let its sap rise once again, unseen, valiant? Behold its glory now, alone, rooted to the same slope of field, its blossoms waving in the breeze.

Plate 33

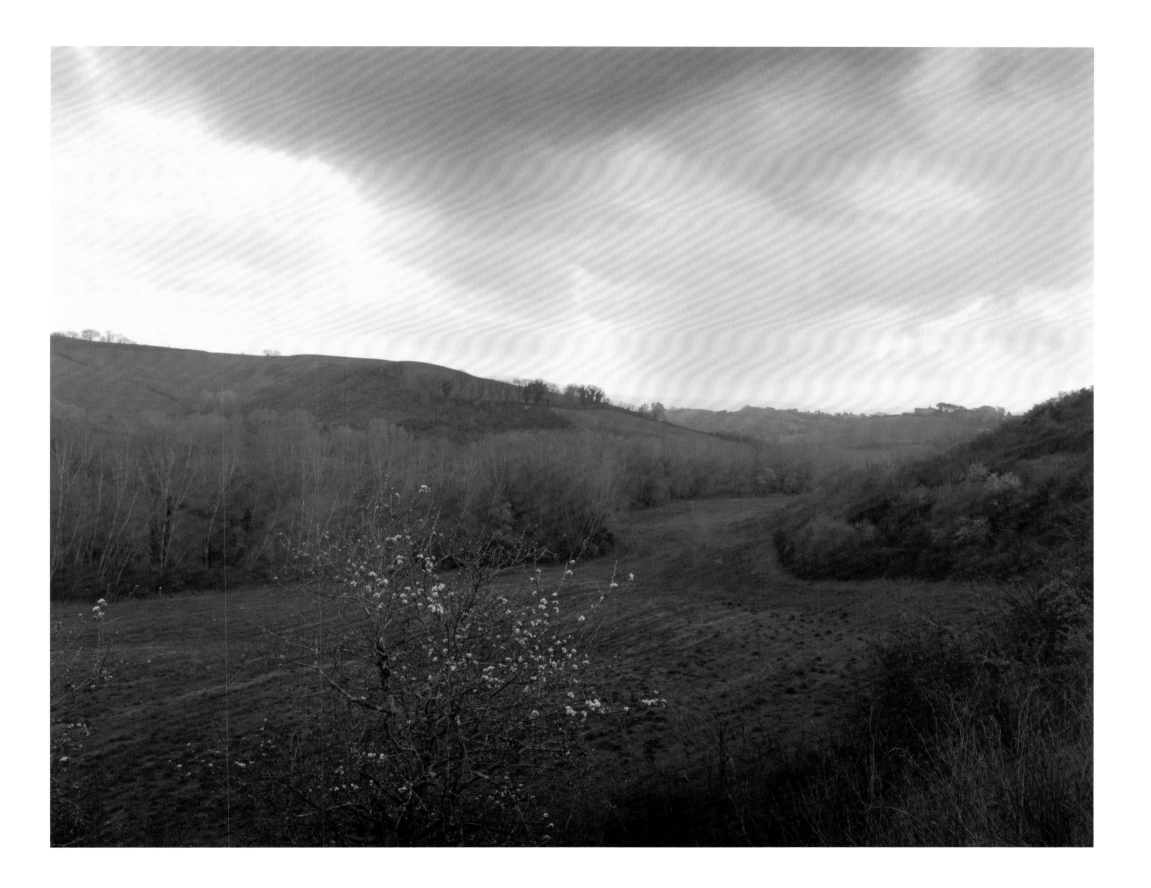

PLATE 34
OVERLEAF: PLATES 35, 36, AND 37

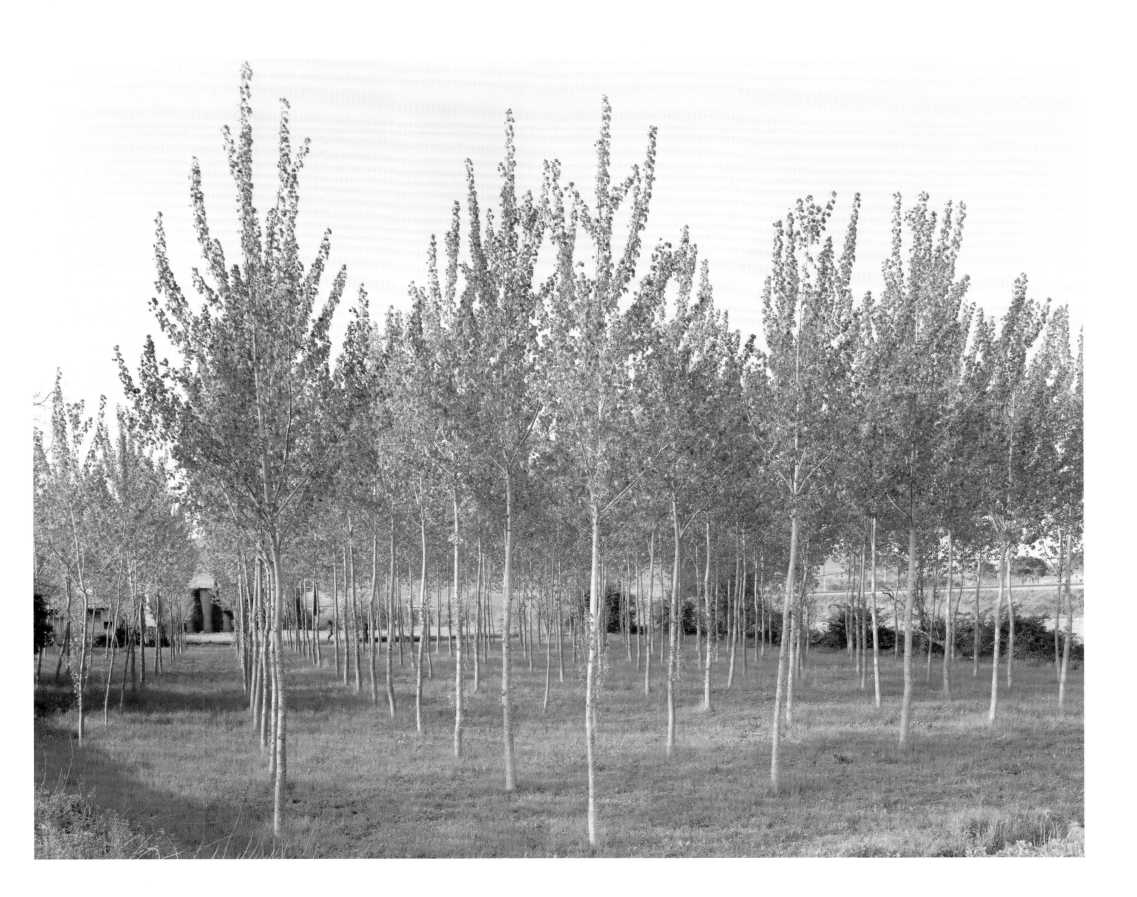

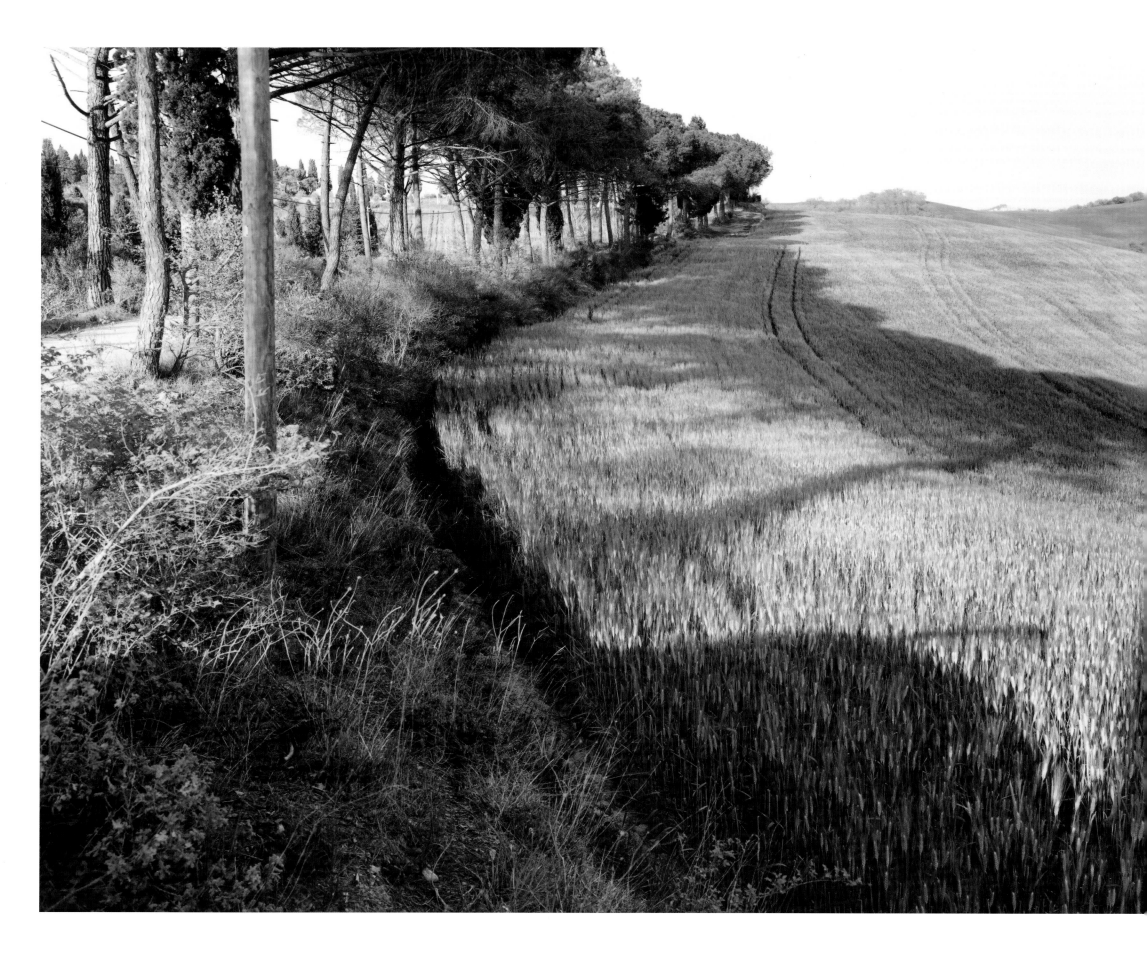

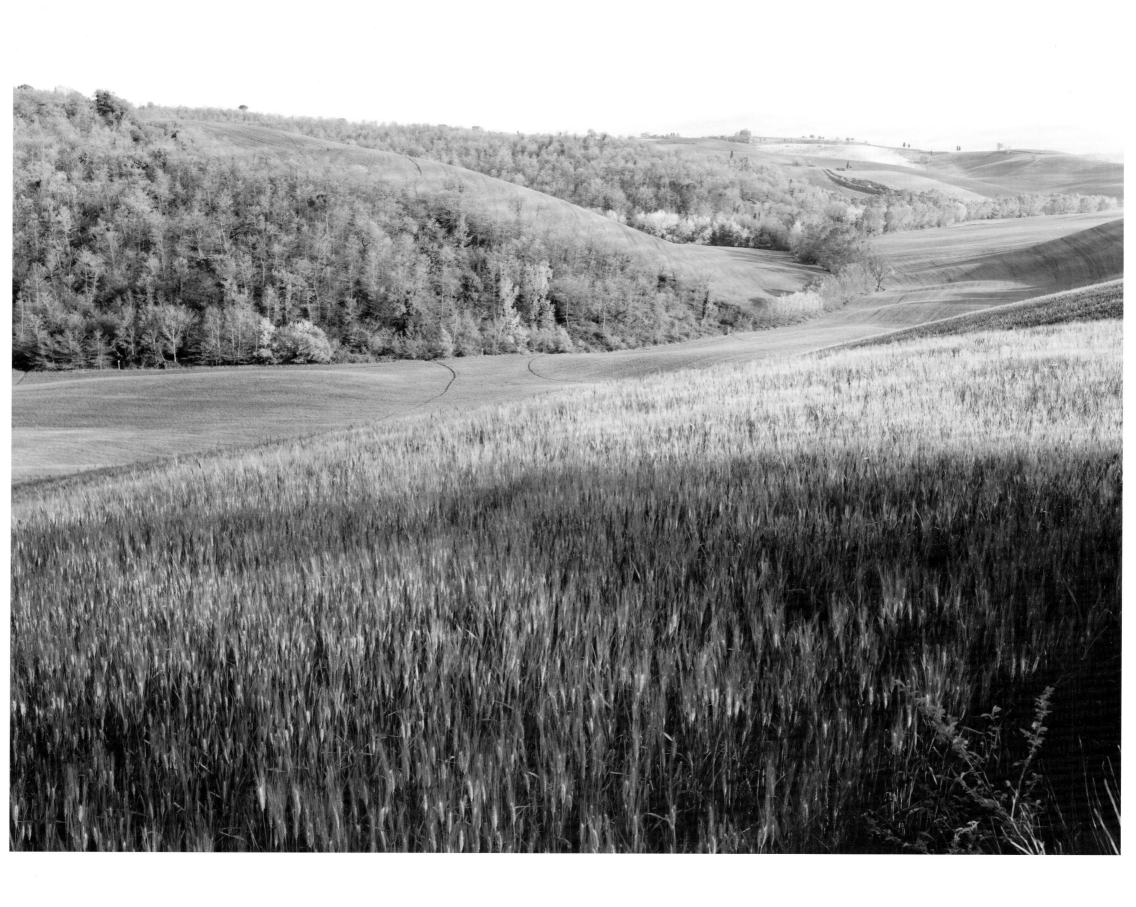

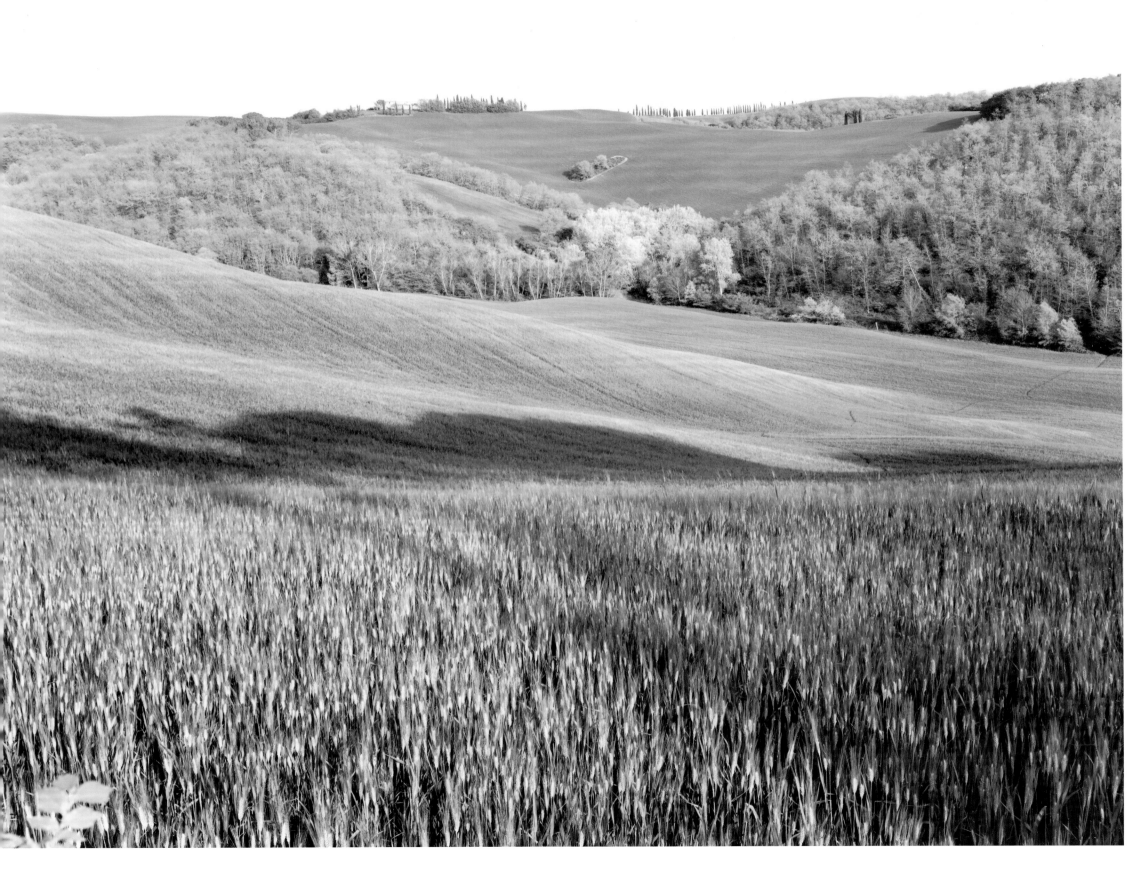

The poppies are coming, their bloody heads pricking the landscape. And so spring journeys, emerging from winter with snowy blossoms of hawthorn, progressing through an enviable vocabulary of greens, and now, finally, the red-hot poppies heralding the arrival of summer. White, green, red…Italy's flag plucked straight from the earth.

PLATE 38
OVERLEAF: PLATES 39 AND 40

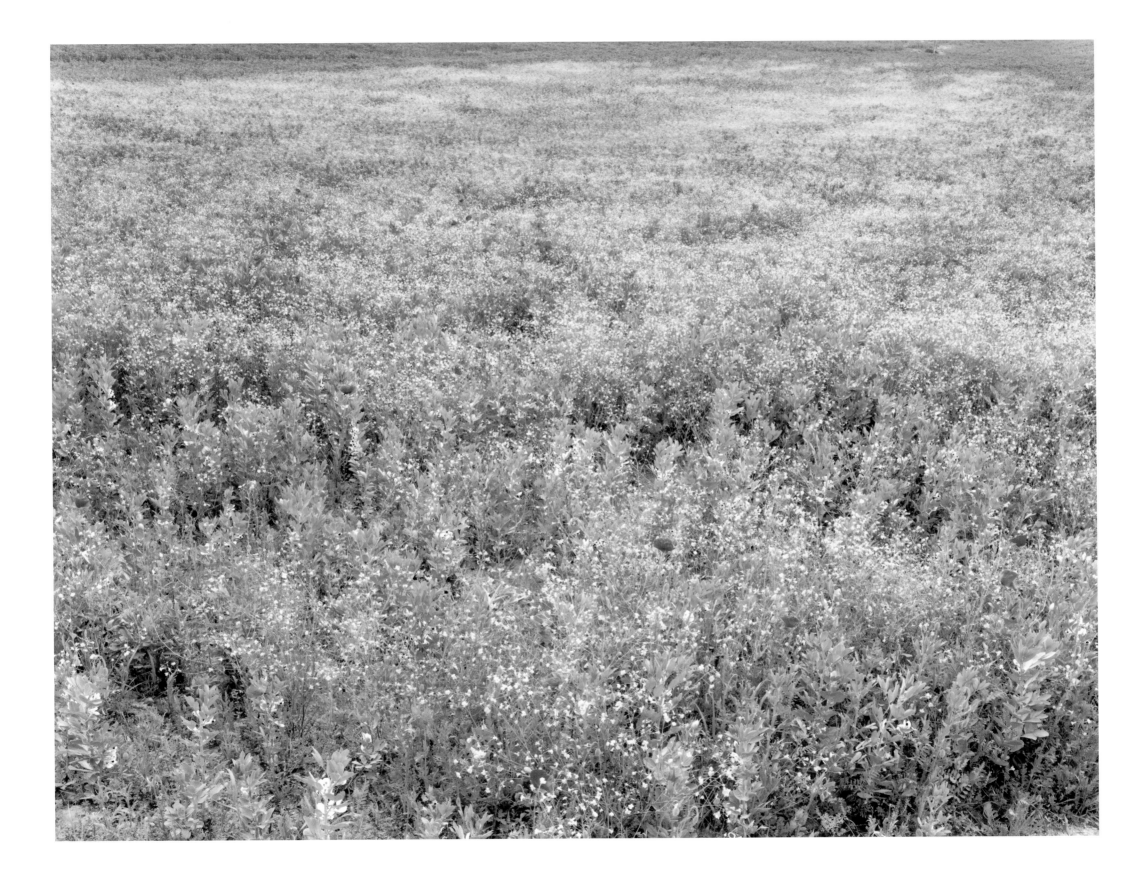

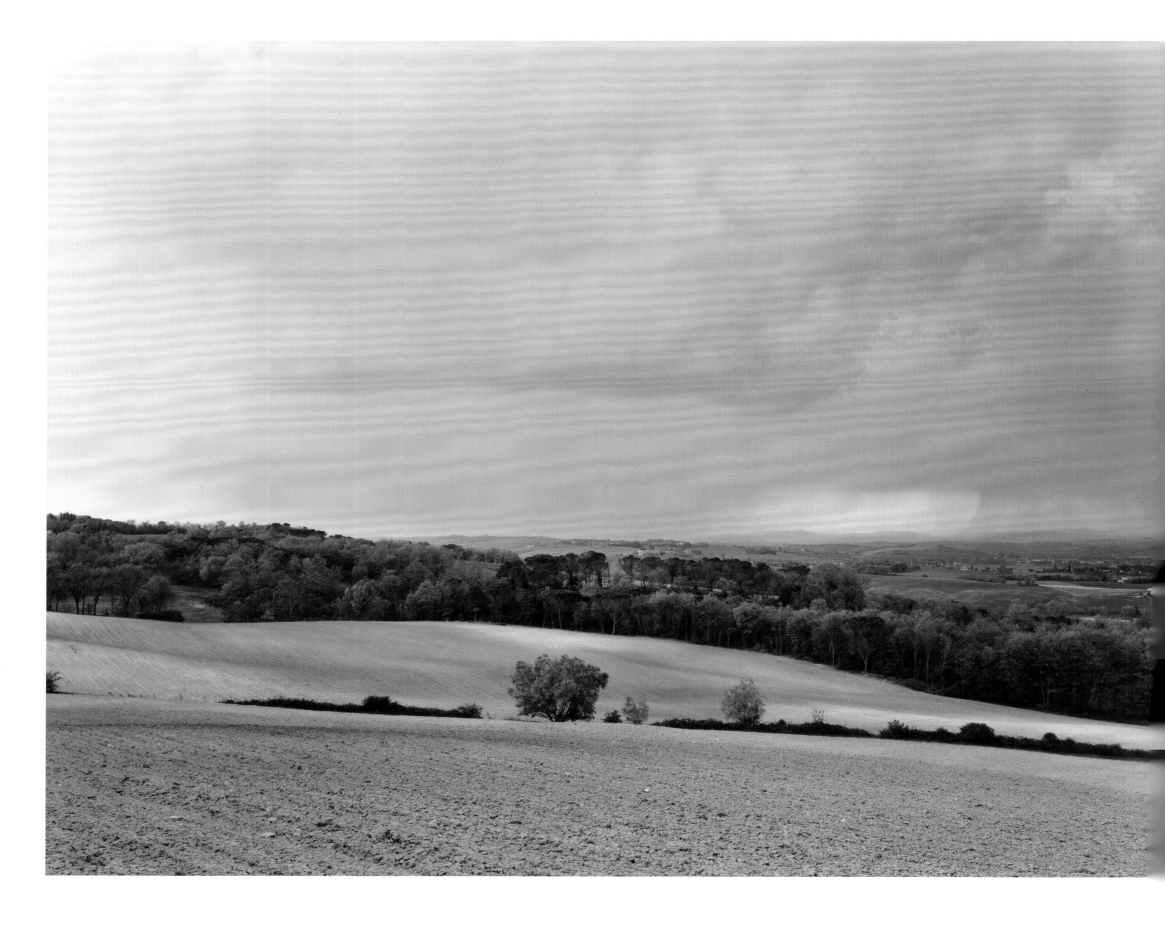

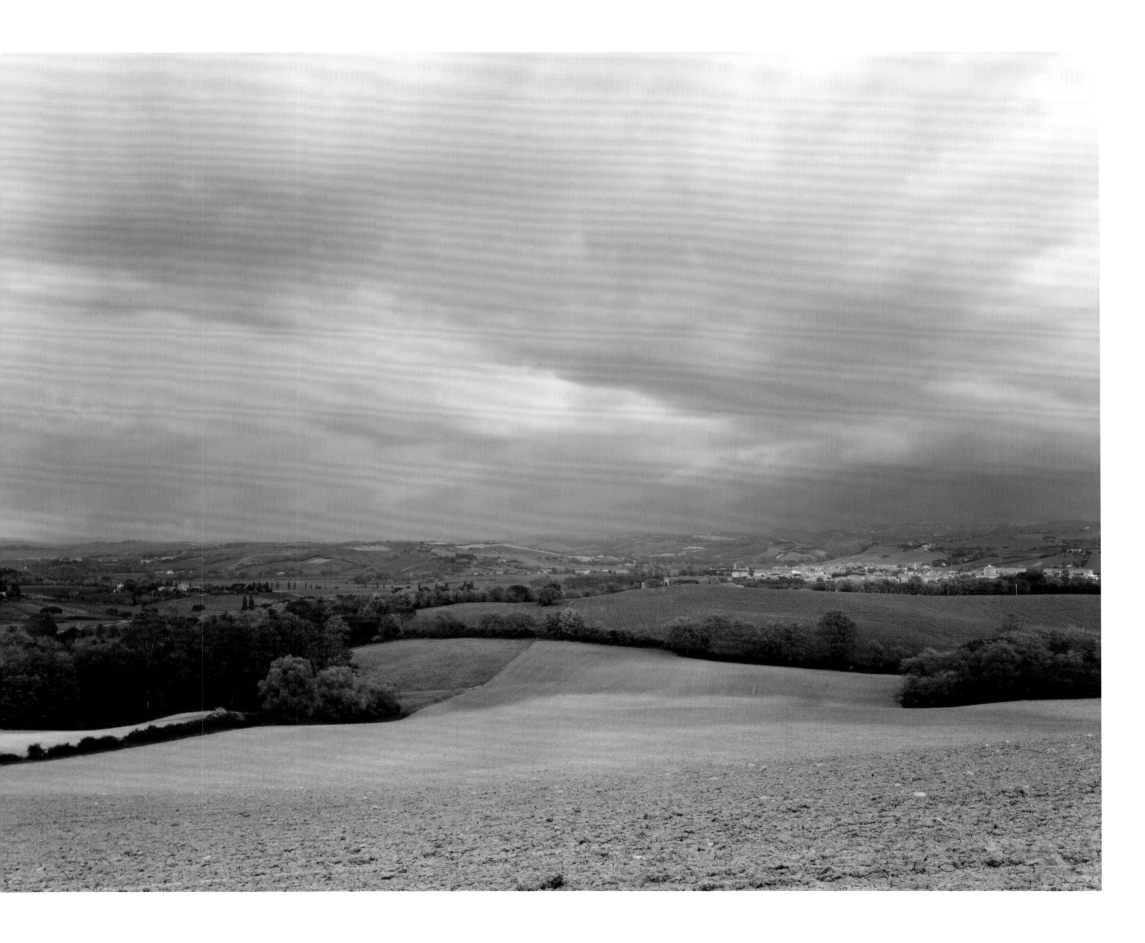

PLATE 41

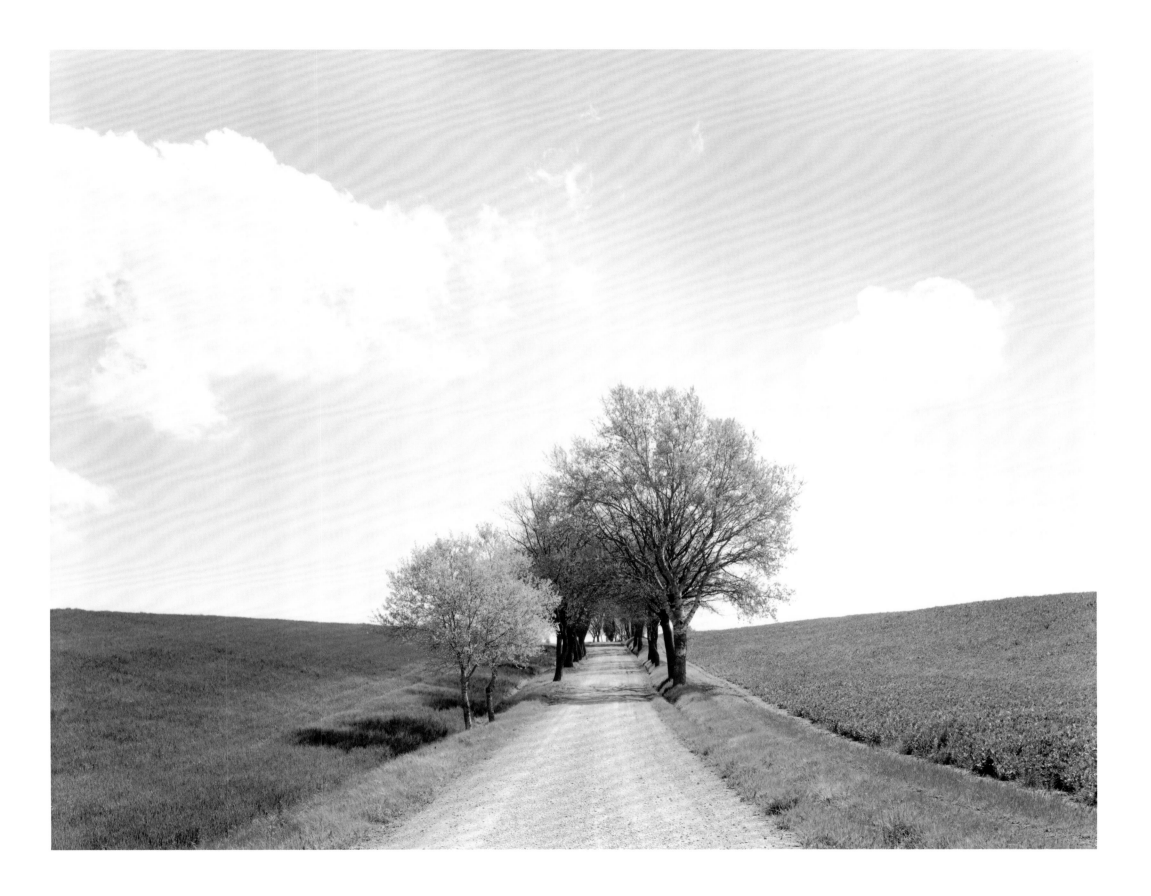

PLATE 42

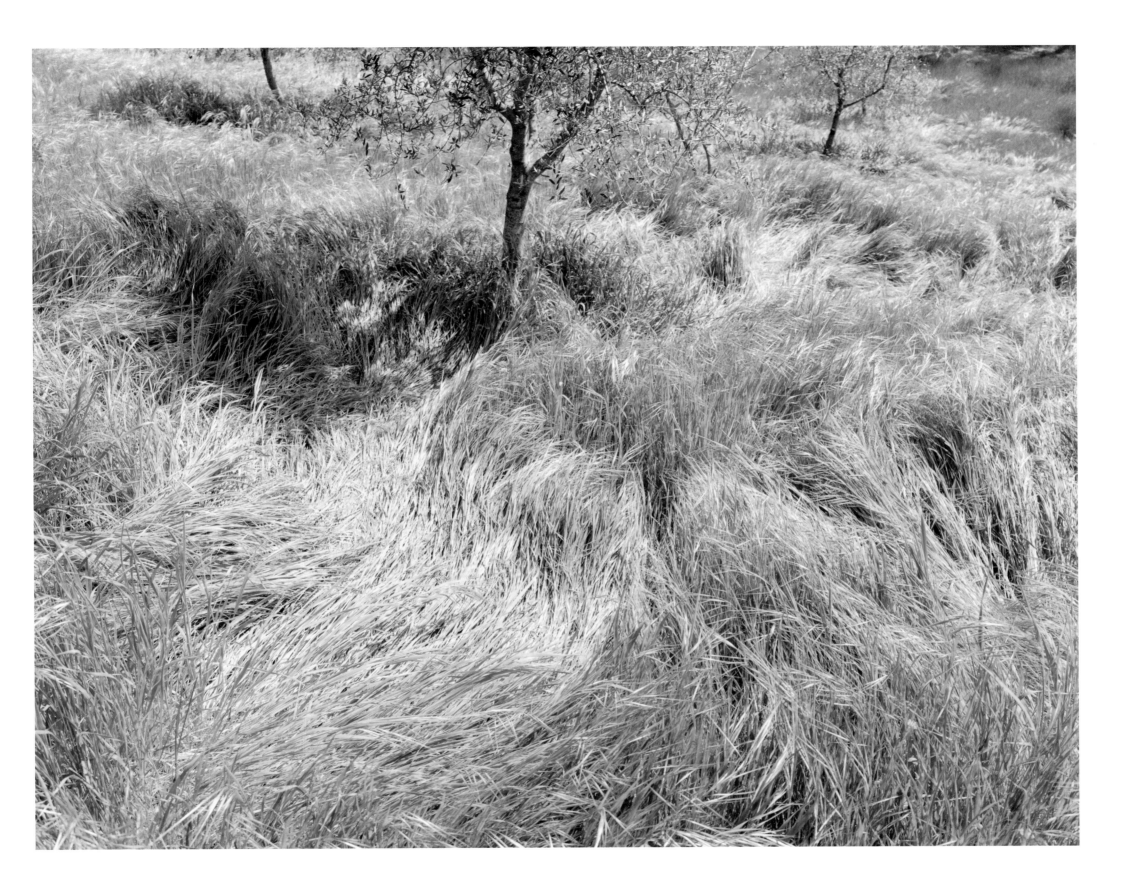

SUMMER

*T*he long shadows of a summer evening meet the

remains of the day's golden light, the wheat lit from deep within. This strawberry blonde crop,

tousled from an afternoon of wind, has come to rest in all its glorious dishevelment beneath the

sky. Ah, summer, season of false eternity, the season that cradles our childhood with some glad

memory of possibility. The length and breadth and depth of those days stay with us forever, as if

the sun had burned the memories into our skin, so that now all one need do is shed a layer of

clothing and feel again the fullness of life.

PLATE 43

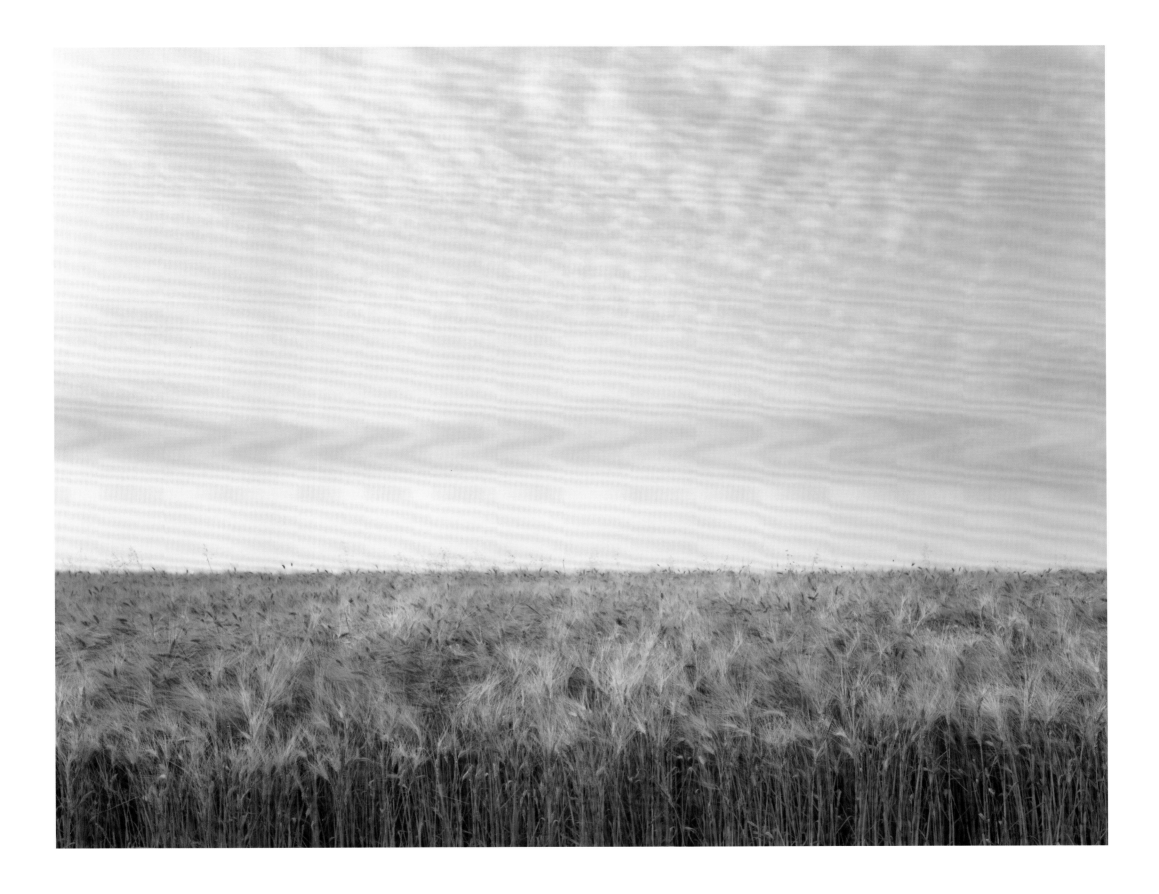

PLATE 44

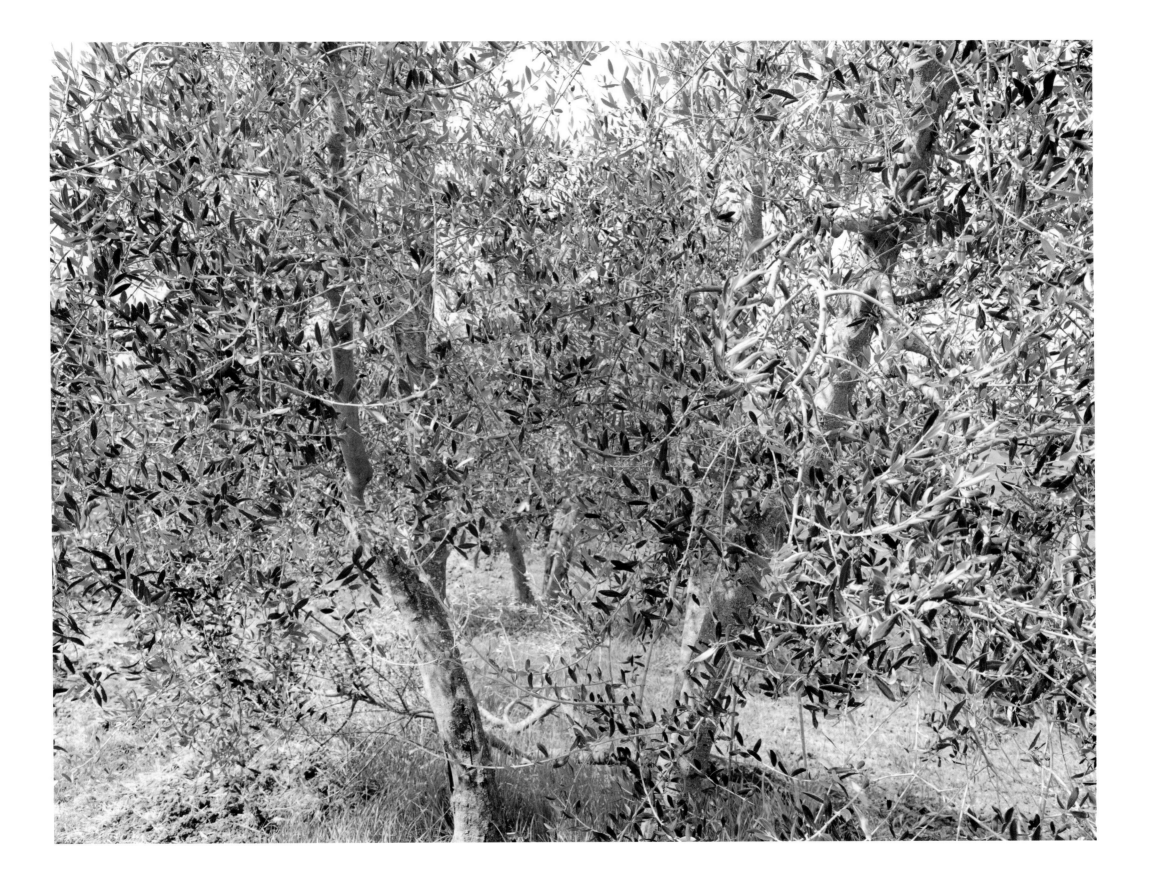

PLATE 45

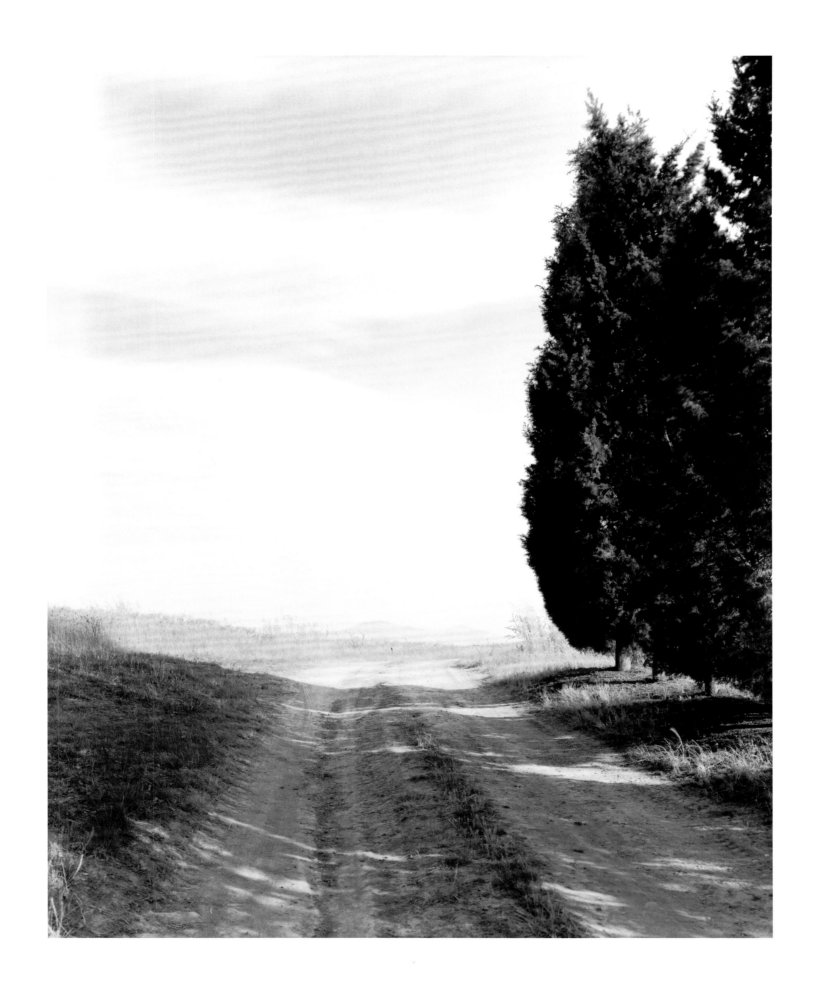

PLATE 46

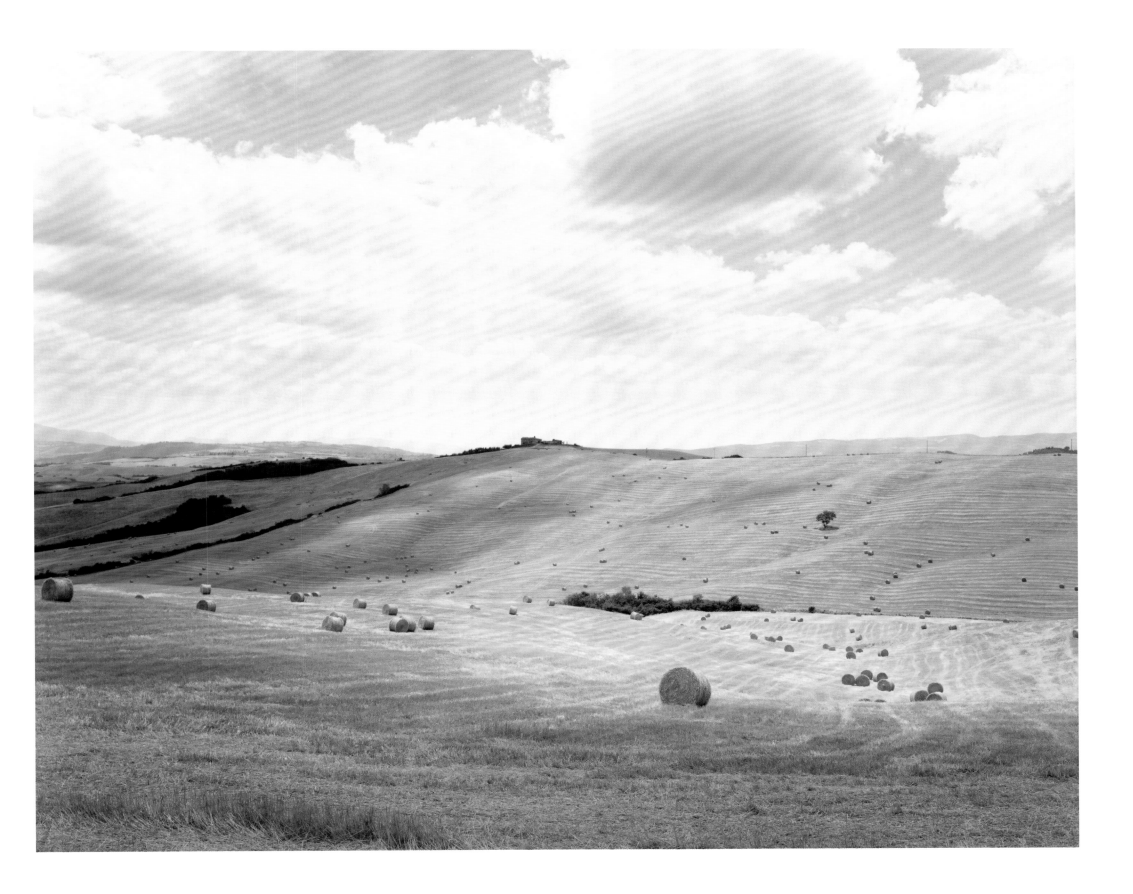

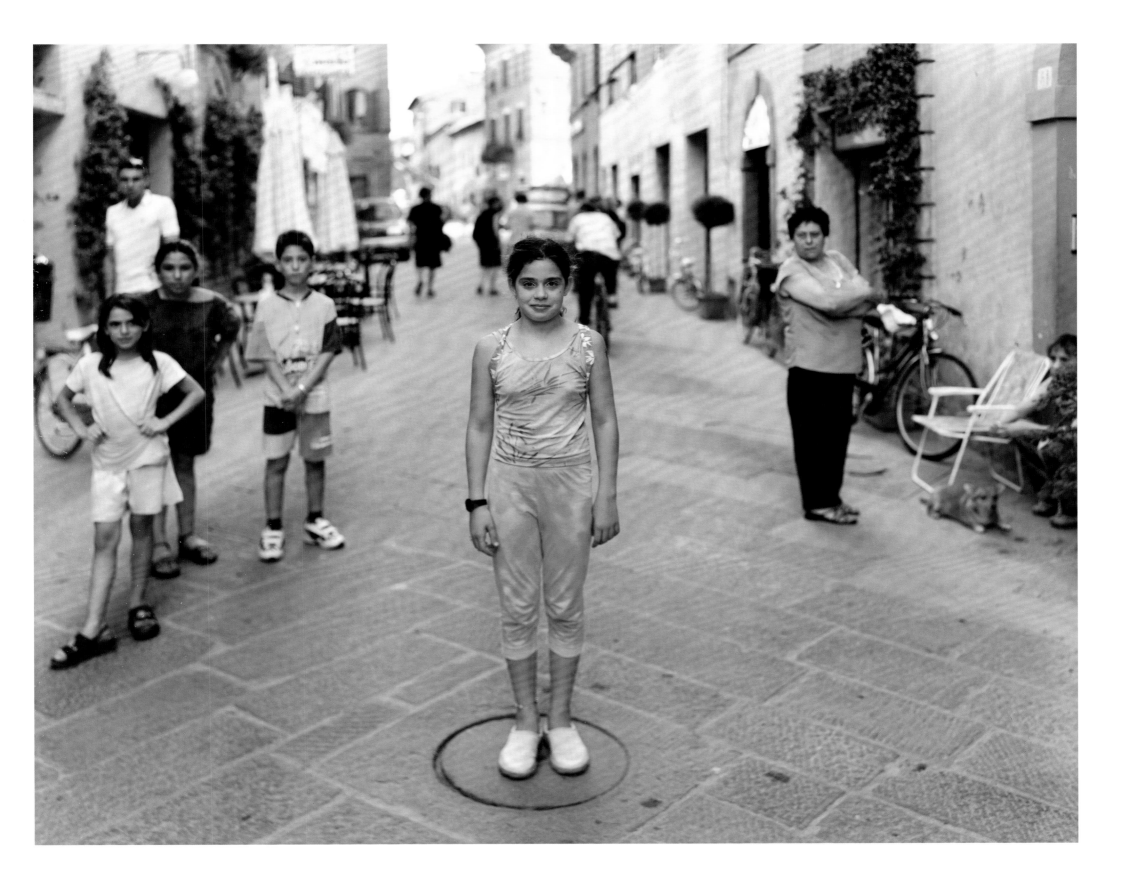

One could write an essay on bicycles, here, where they are still the contemporary horse. Everyone has one. The women in their skirts carry provisions. Teenage boys, practicing for the circus, sometimes carry as many as three or four friends, all hanging off handlebars and saddles…and each other. And there's always a young prince riding past with his princess standing behind him, her hands on his shoulders, her young body like a figure on a ship's bow, poised, hair streaming. In the evening, the older men ride out of town in groups, to admire the sunset. But perhaps my favorites are the young mothers with their toddlers proudly displayed on the handlebars, stopping every few yards down the street to receive the abundant, daily admiration of their produce. It's all here, light, shadow, youth, age…here, and then gone.

PLATE 48

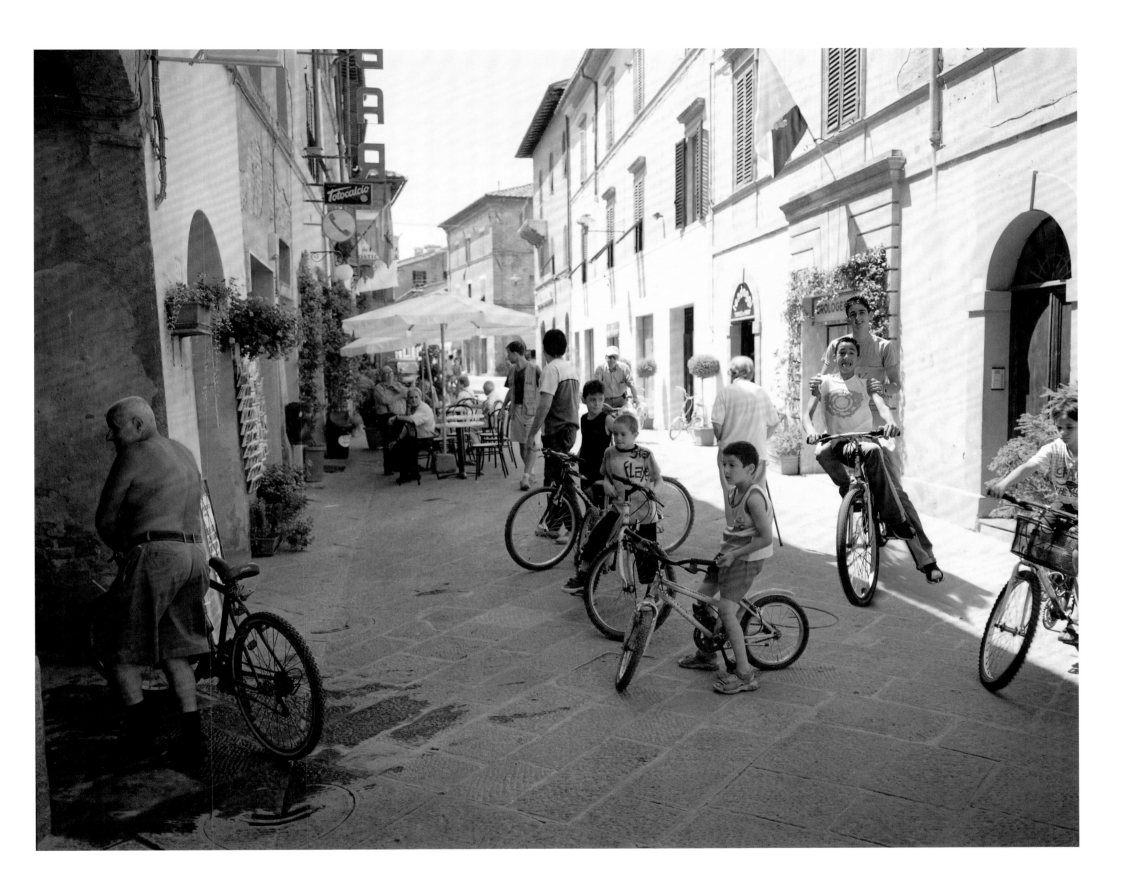

PLATE 49

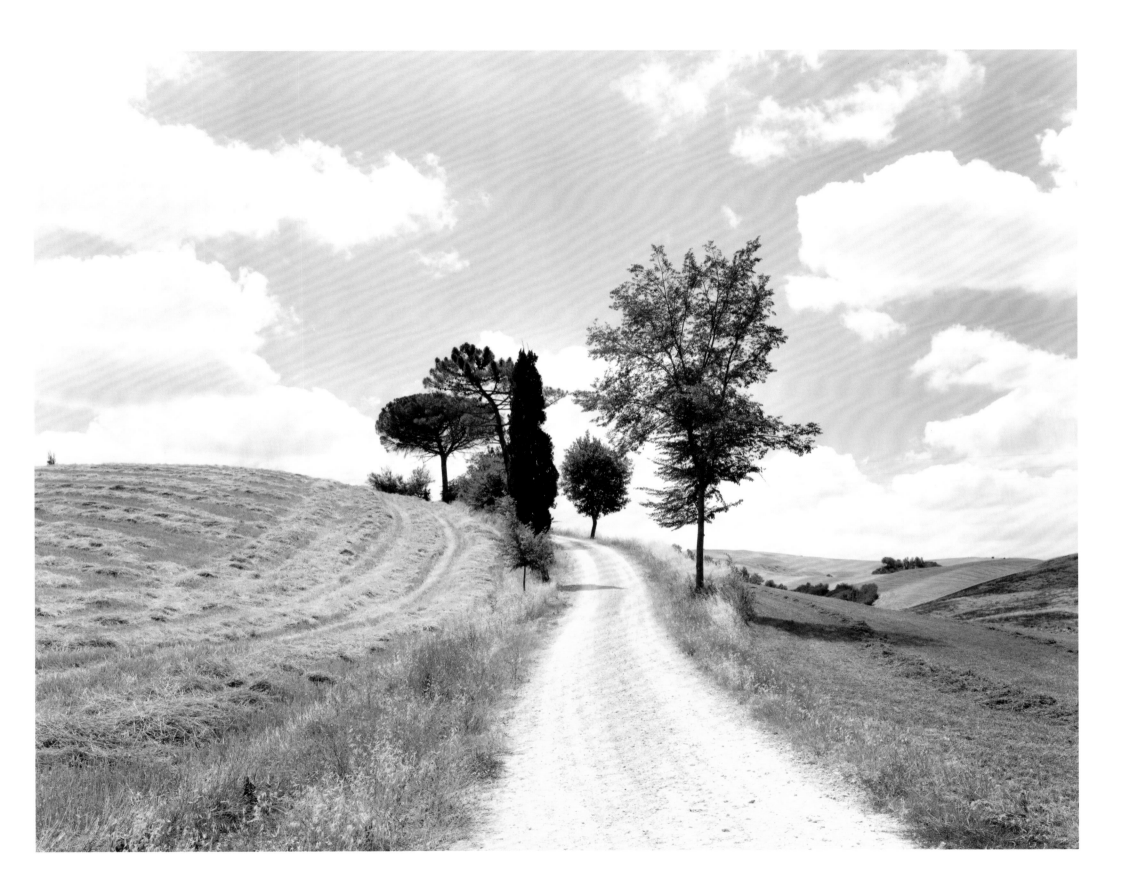

PLATE 50

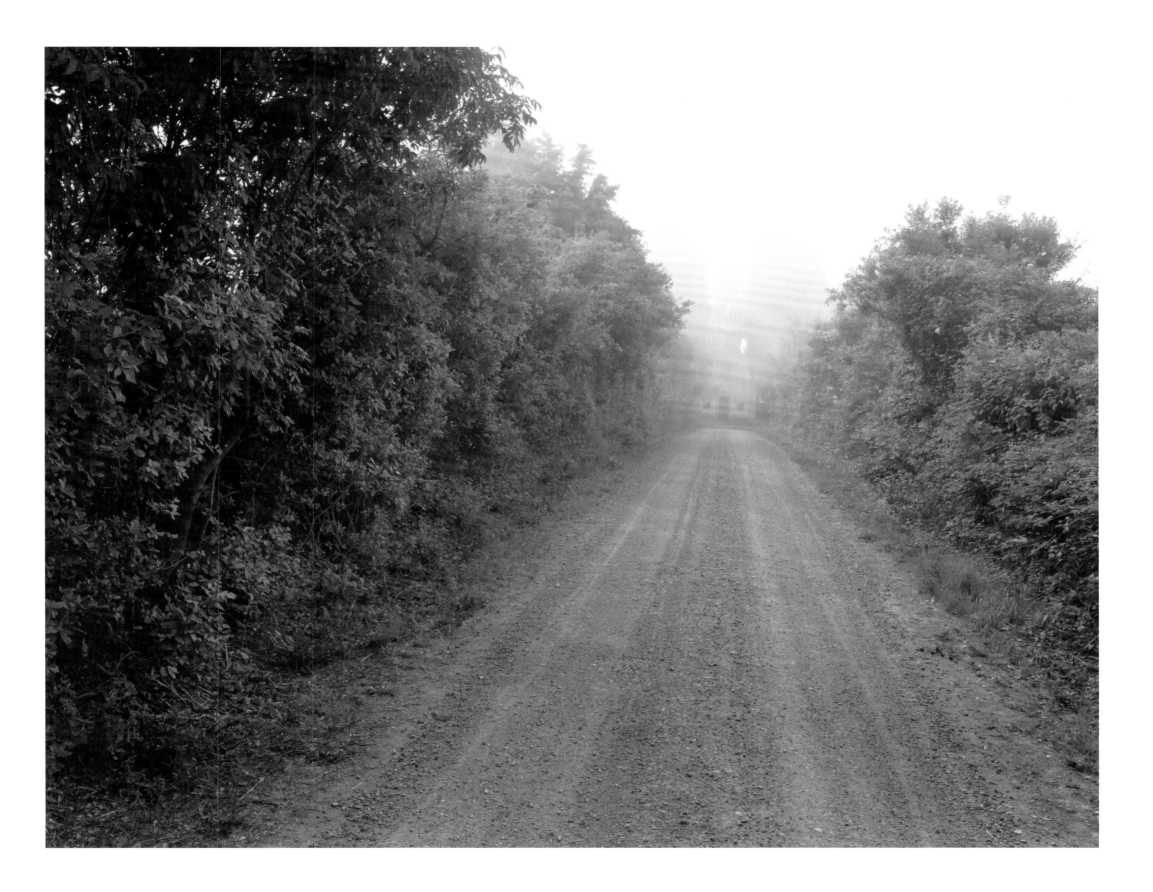

PLATE 51

OVERLEAF: PLATES 52 AND 53

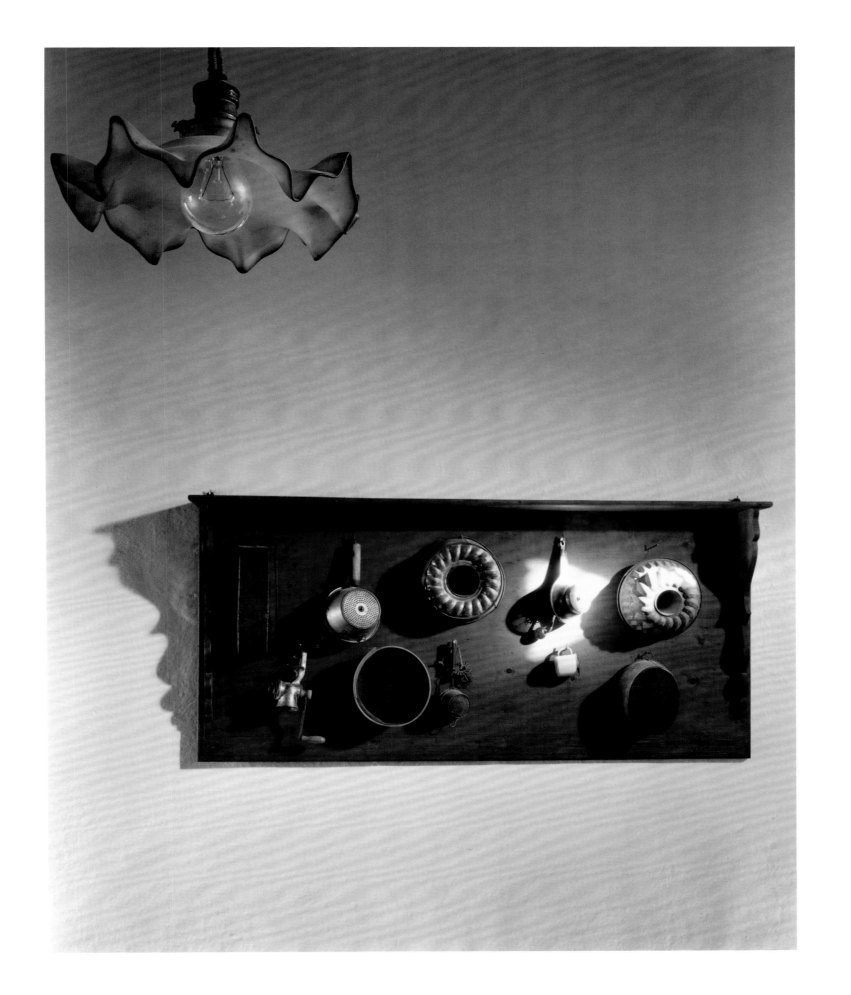

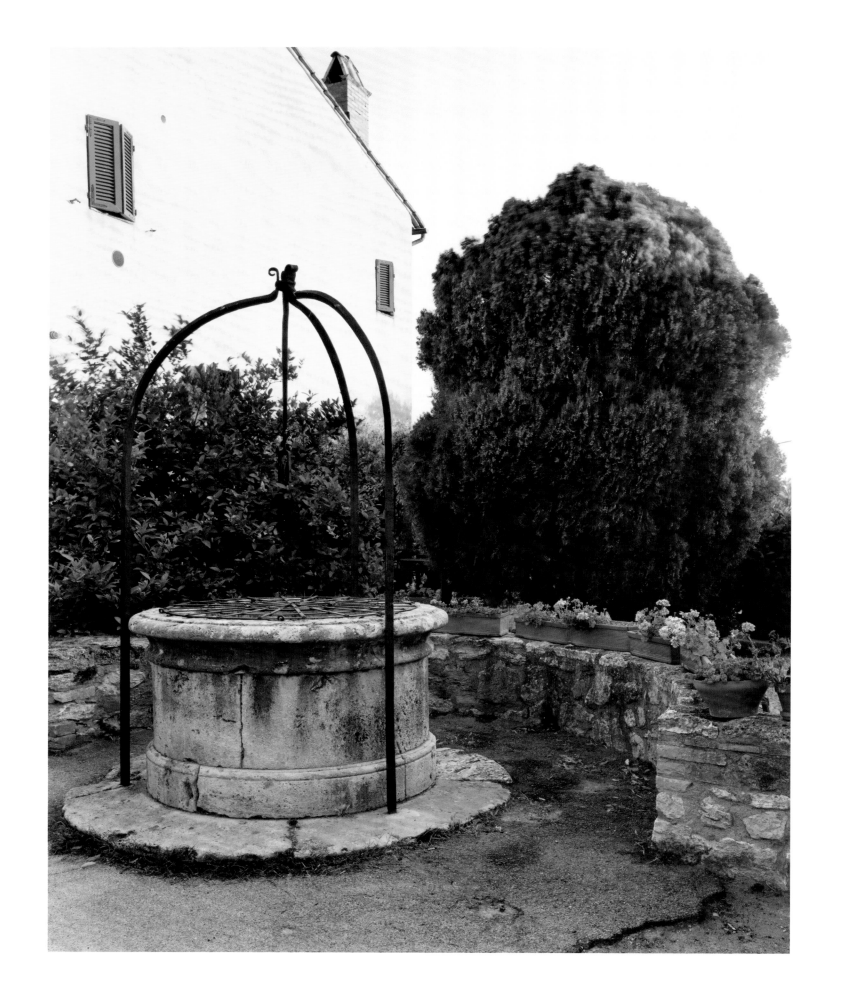

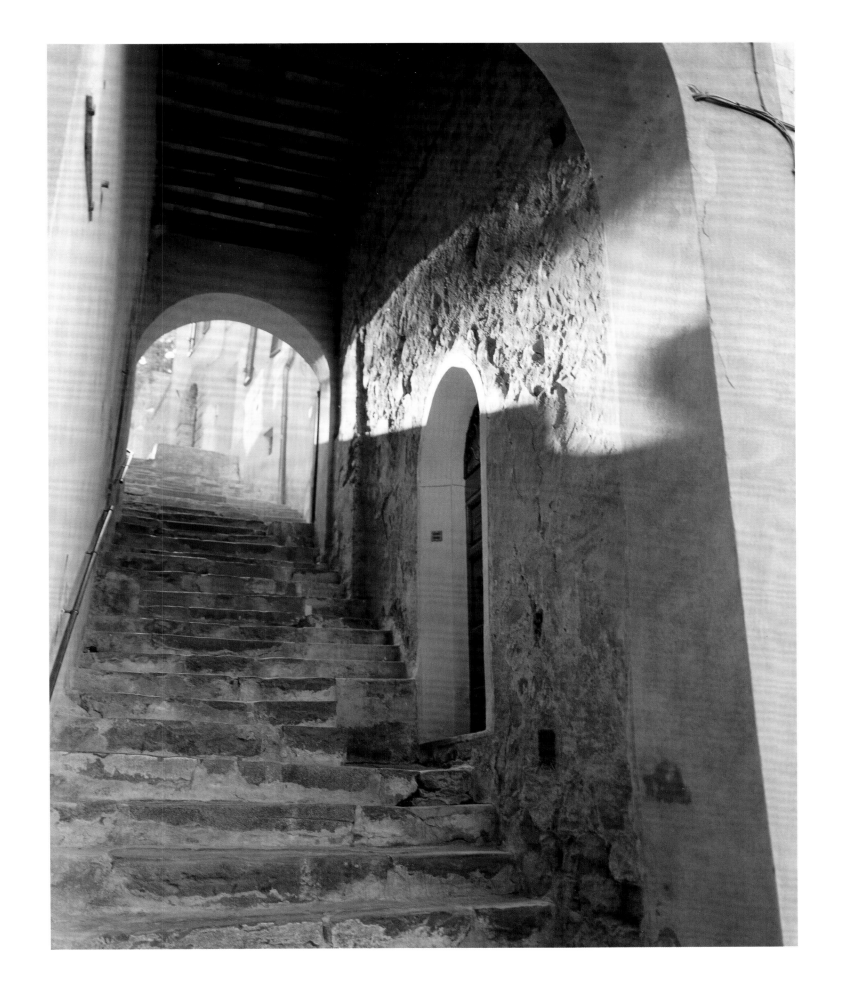

*T*here are moments and places like this where nature is still so awesome that we experience ourselves cut down to size. Yet the experience is not one of diminishment, but of relief and harmony. To feel oneself in direct relationship to the planet is to experience a profound connection, and in these moments we understand the true meaning of belonging.

PLATE 54

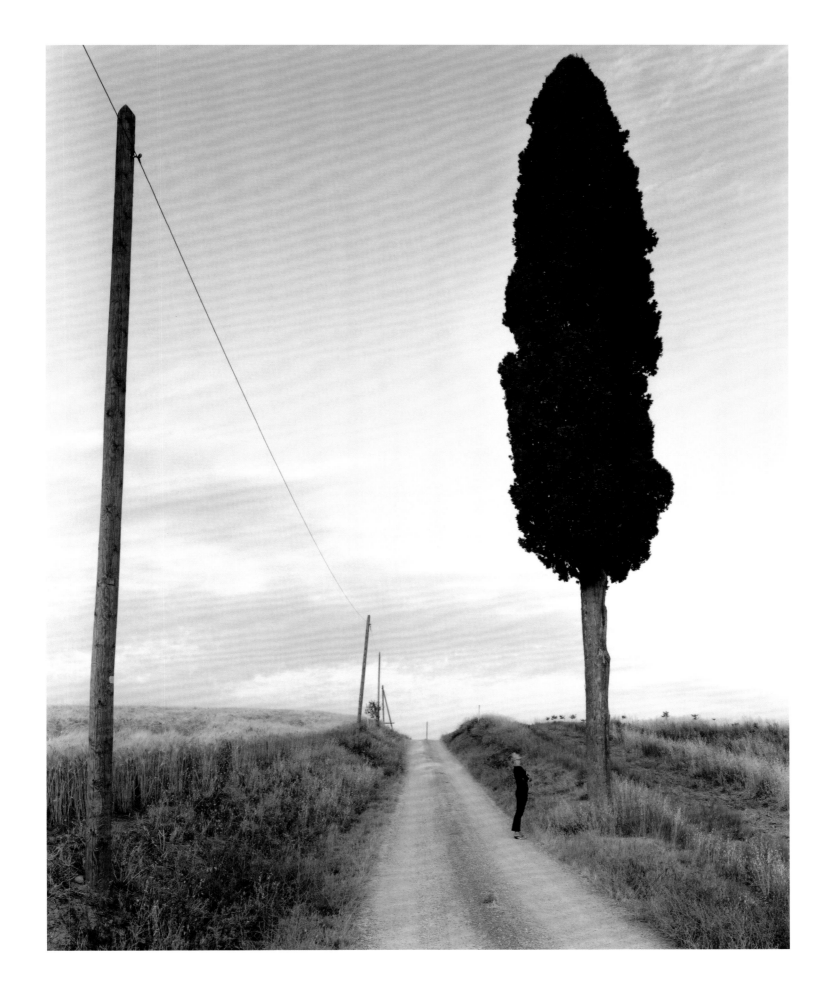

PLATE 55

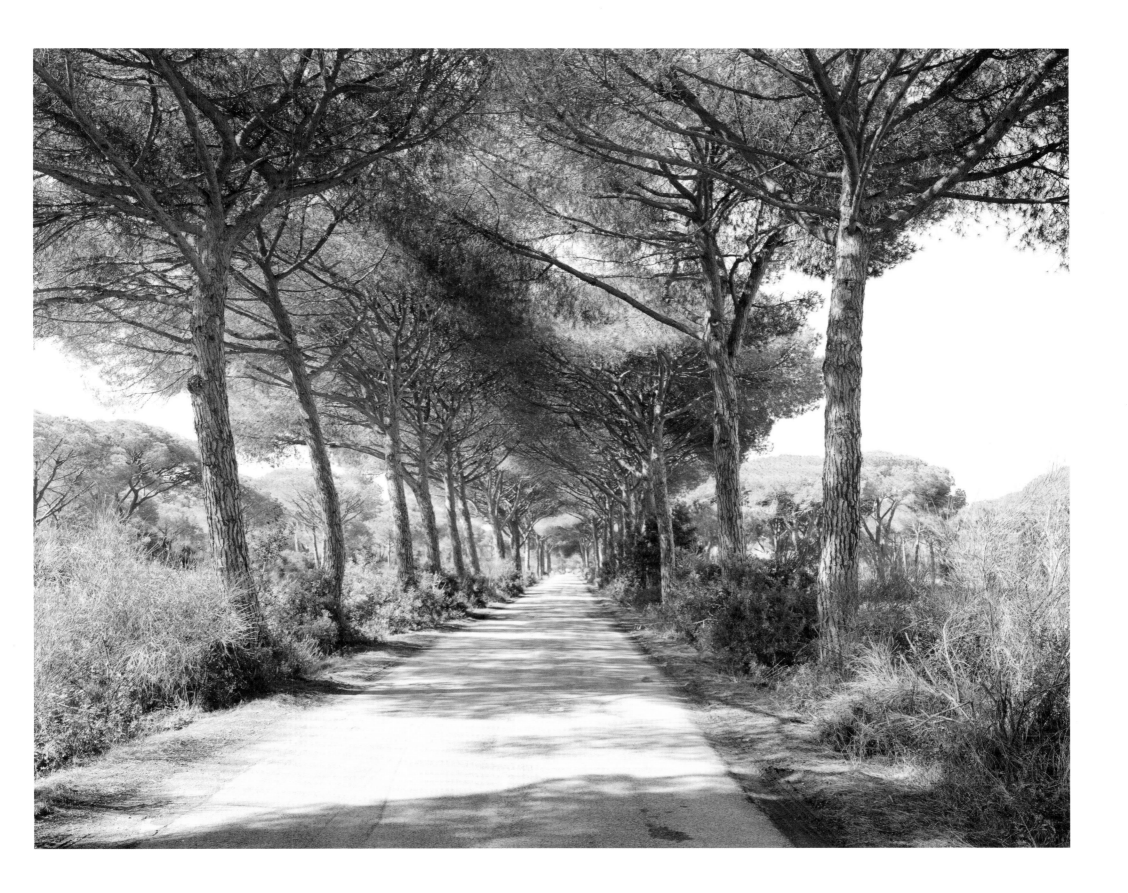

PLATE 56

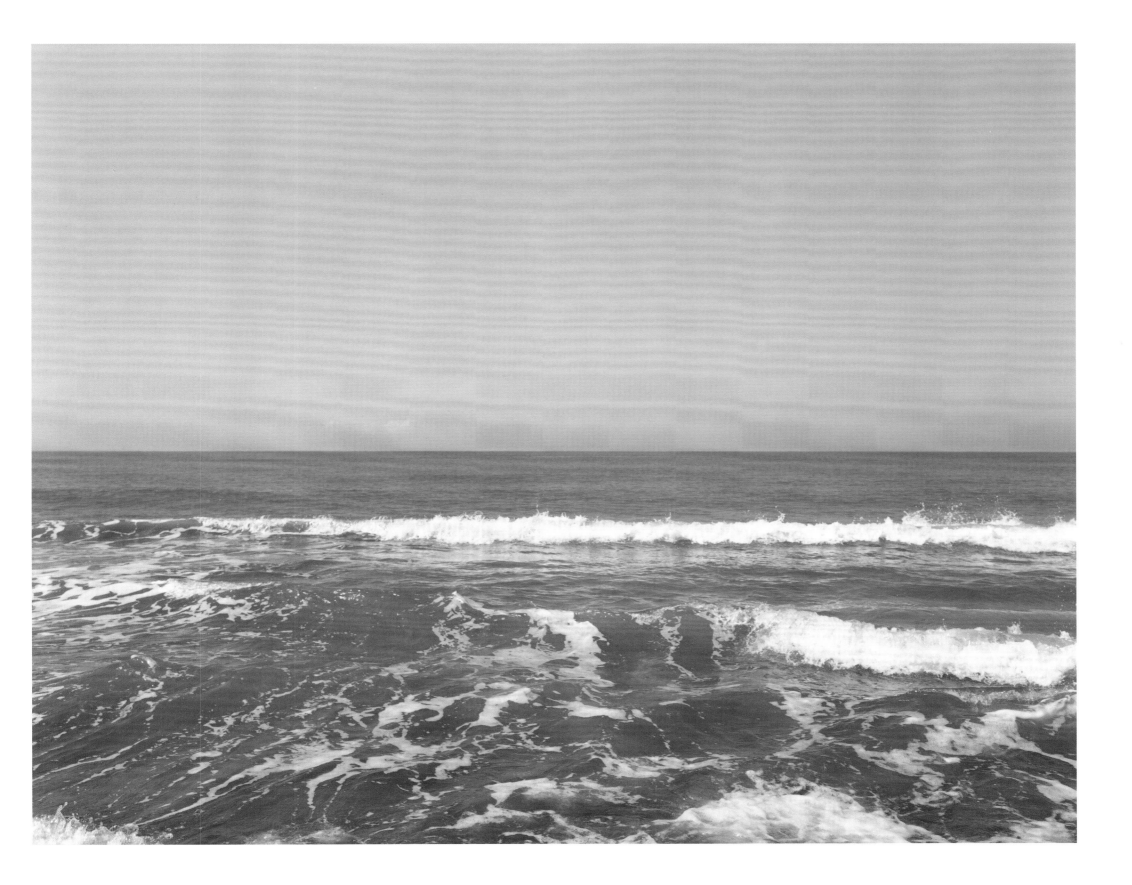

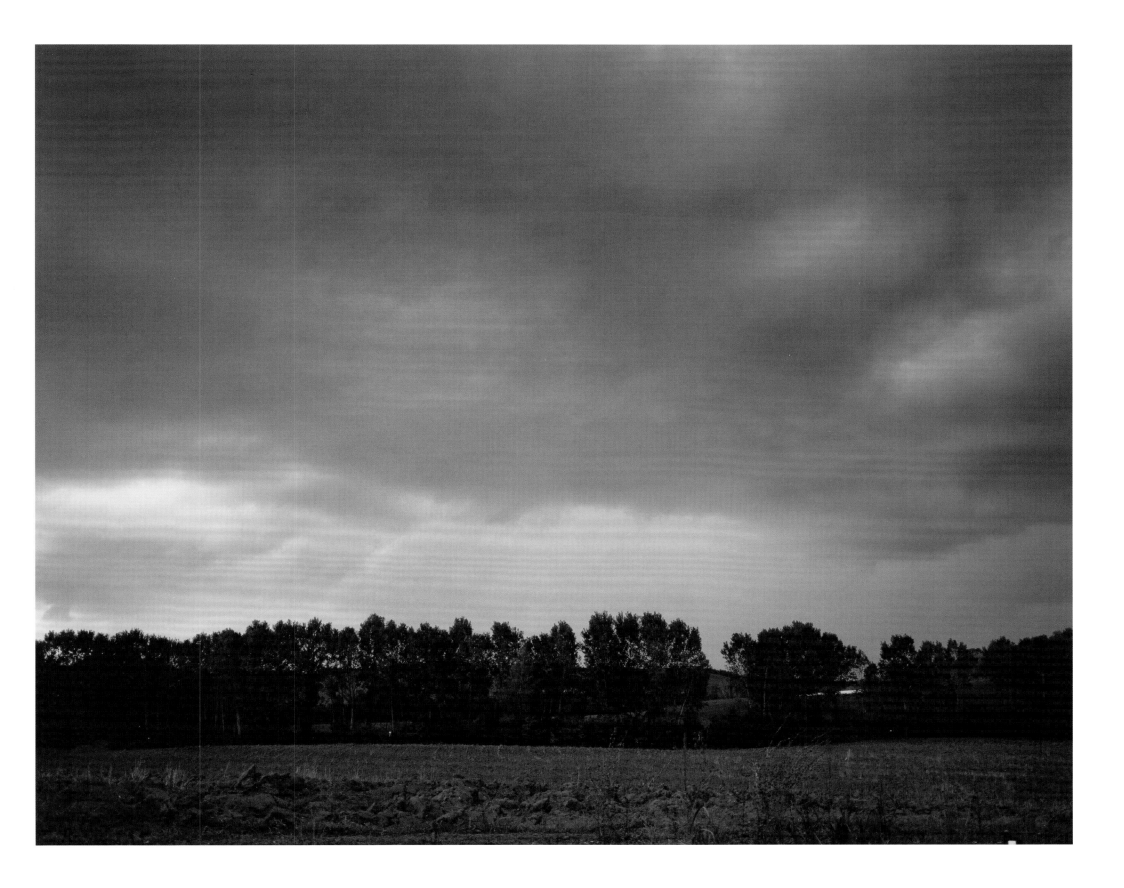

AUTUMN

*T*hey call him Peppo. He tells us he is gleaning the cobs to feed his animals and we are reminded, once again, of the life lived in honor of, and participation with, the cycles of the earth. Then he tells us he was a prisoner of war. Five years, in Germany. He tells us this in the same manner he tells of feeding his animals. His face is benign. We try to imagine his return to this, after five years like that. It is obvious the two things don't go together. His son comes over to say hello. This is my father, he says, he was a prisoner of war, five years.

PLATE 58

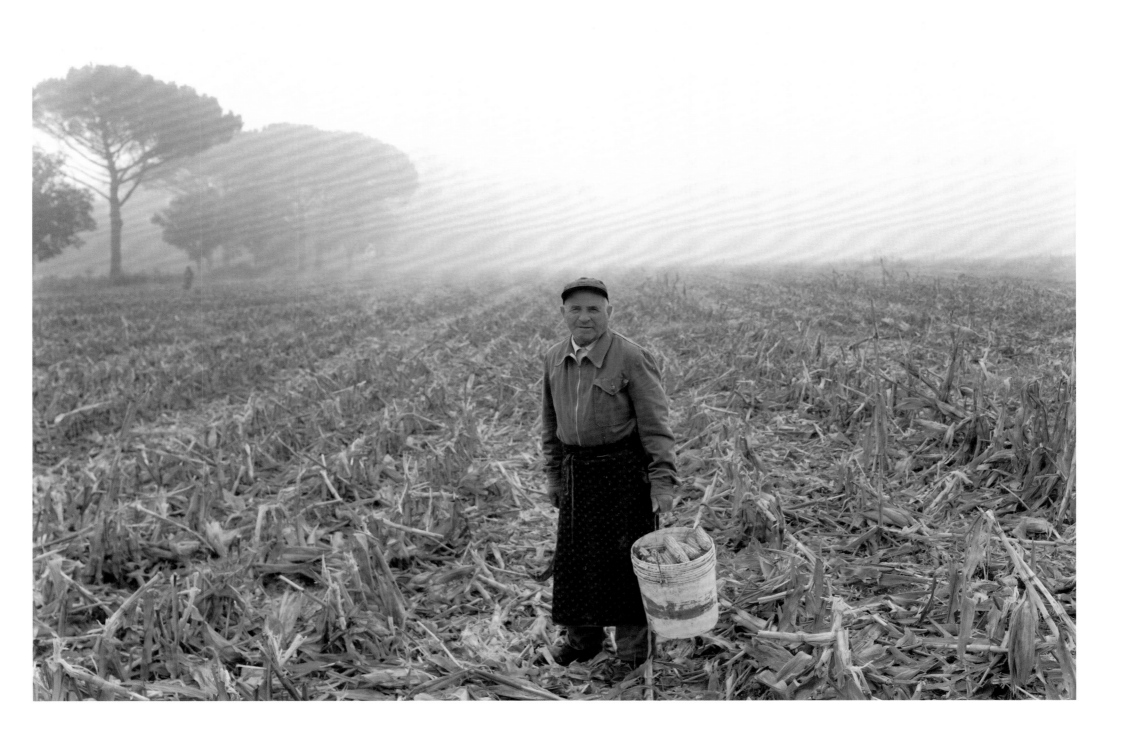

PLATE 59

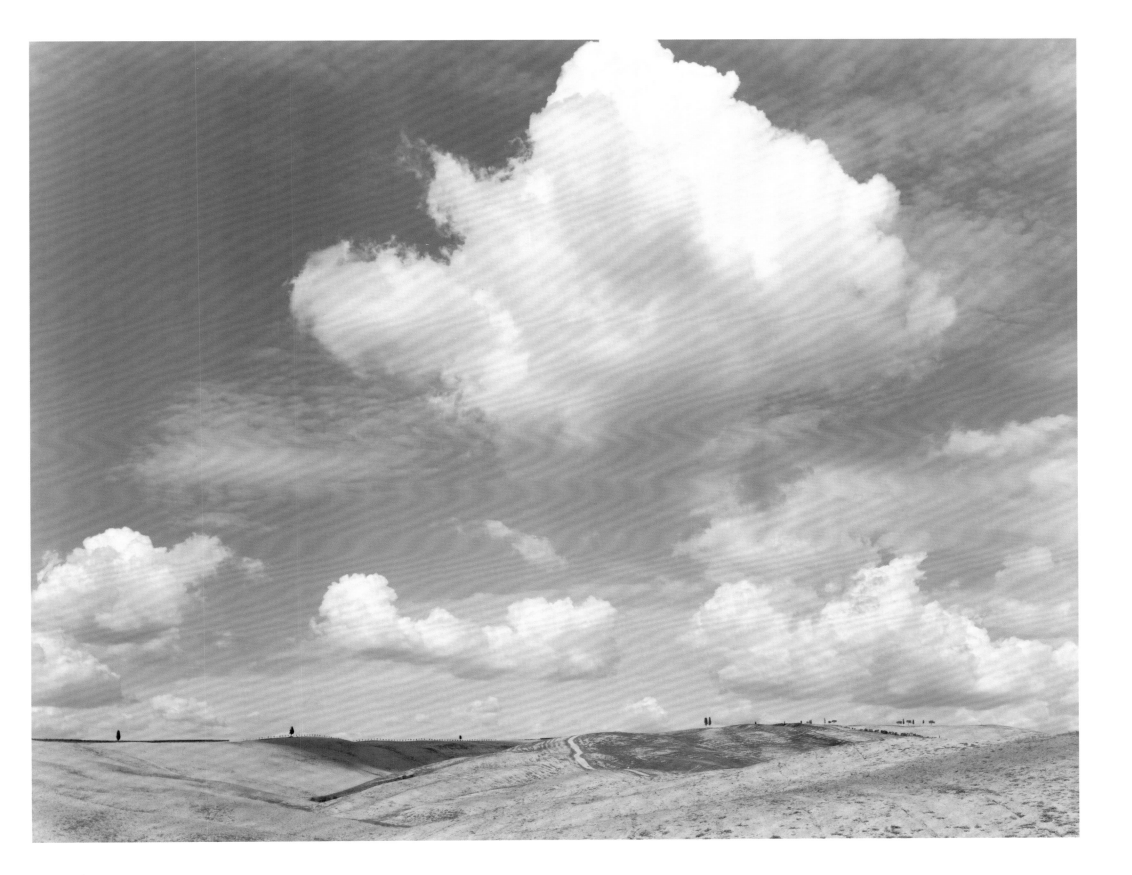

*J*oel has been making a photograph of the complexity and harmony of buildings, light, shadow, and our favorite linden tree. I sit beside him on a small flight of steps, dreaming, gazing, and thinking I should be writing. But I seem unable to put into words what I have been struggling to say all year. It is about the complexity of harmony that I have been trying to write: that particular musical quality that marries notes in such a way as to describe humanity's desire and sorrow. And now I see it before me, there in the drainpipe that pours itself down in a stream of color exactly matching that of the brick walkway it barely touches, the bricks fitting into each other like the spine of a sardine. And this dusty, faded color, the color of very old blood, runs down to a compressed pile of grape skins, the juice of which now sits in a vat awaiting its time of ferment. The pile of skins, which is both waste and the shape of things to come, resonates with the brick and the drainpipe and a lone patch of stucco on the wall behind it. This interweaving of necessity creates a harmony that is both simple and intricate. It is a small passage in the symphony of centuries of toil, composed by the generations who have truly lived here.

PLATE 60

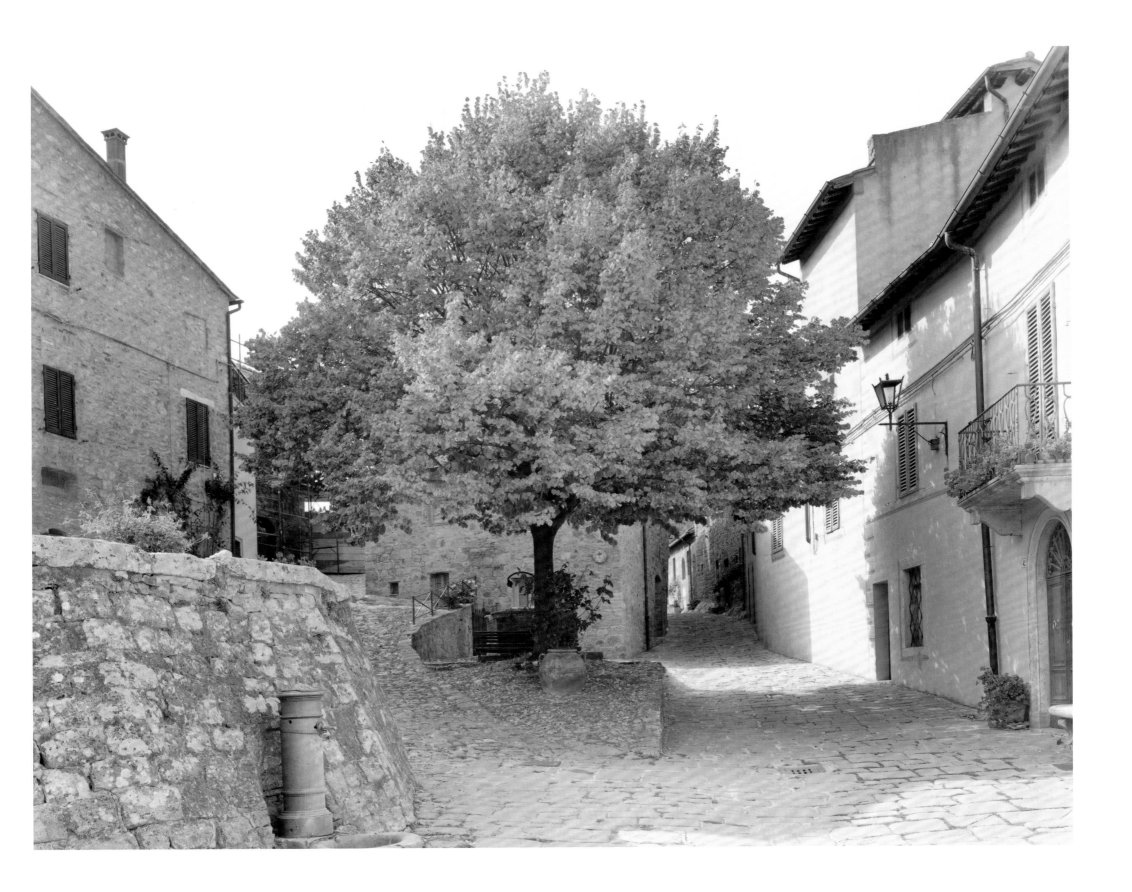

Plate 61

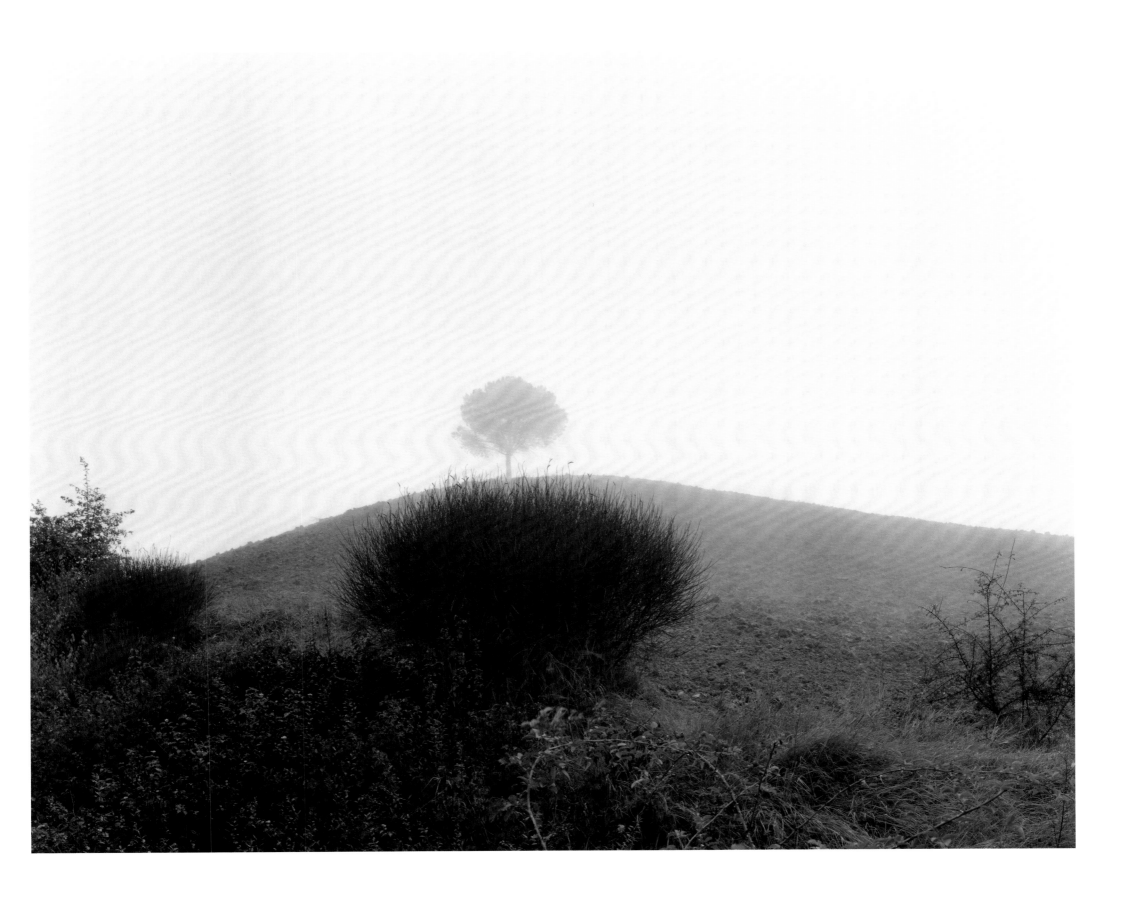

*T*he *sagra* is over. Nine days of ritual in homage to the

bounty of the land, and everywhere you look there is food. During this time the town experiences

a spirit of community that is its true bounty, and we are left with everlasting images. The surprise

of rounding a corner to see a street filled with tables. A seventy-year-old woman standing over an

enormous pot of polenta, stirring it with a spoon the size of a spade; just standing, staring, stirring, in

the corner of a furious kitchen. A boy's unlined face beaming with the joy of life, the way it will fifty

years hence. Teenagers—pierced and tattooed like the rest of the world's youth—carrying trays of

food with a good will that belies the belligerence of their fashion. An eighty-year-old woman, tiny at

the sink, working her way through stacks of dirty plates with all the concentration of a Zen monk.

Floriana, standing up at her table in the packed courtyard singing like a six-year-old. Lisena, her white

cap atilt, feeding us straight from the fire.

PLATE 62

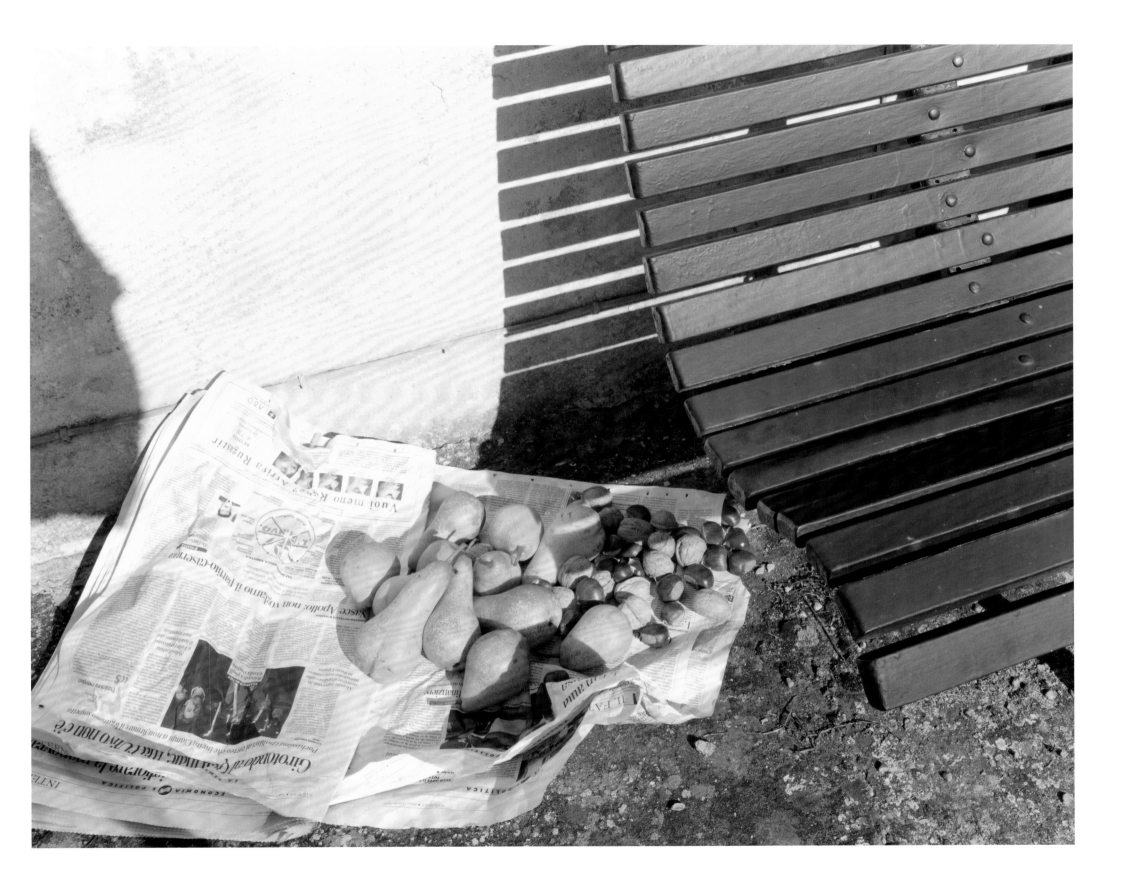

PLATE 63

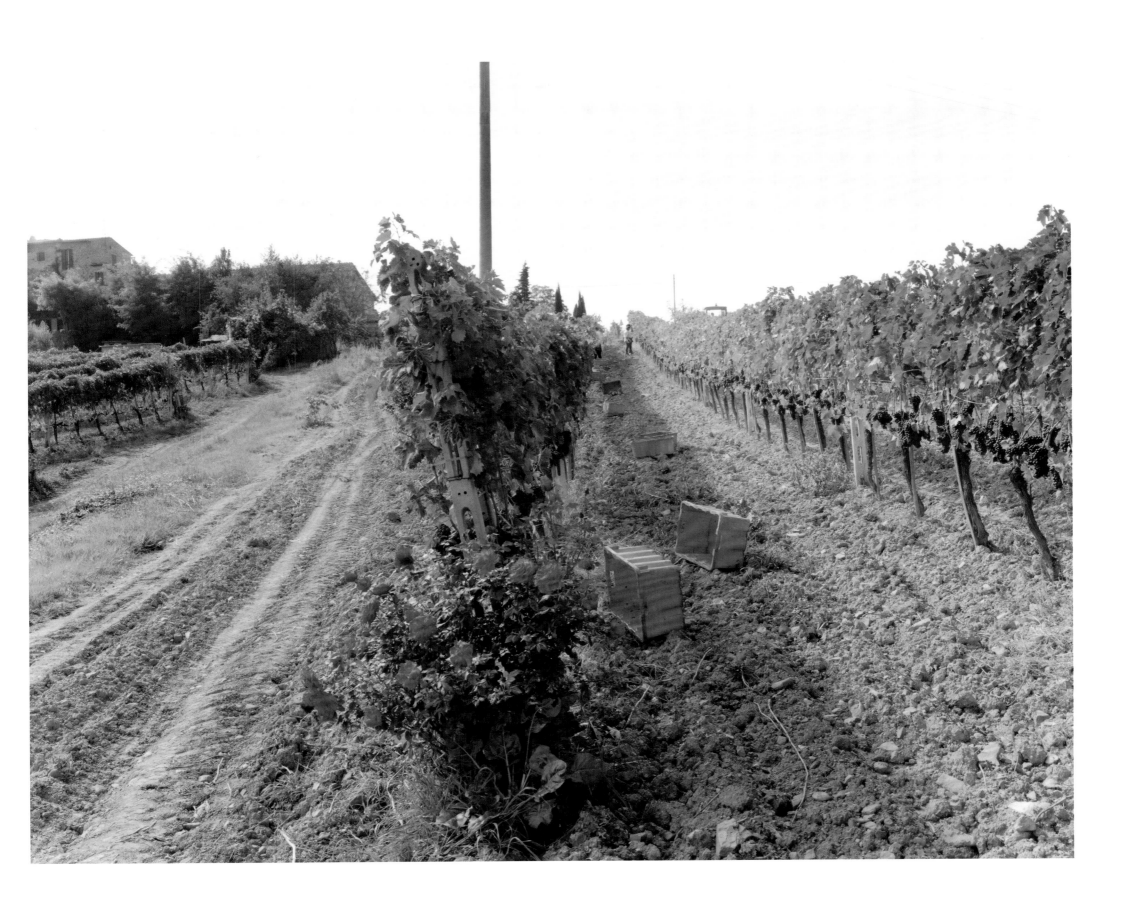

A Harvest Lunch

Pane

Pasta con lepre

Potate con formaggio e prosciutto

Focaccia

Pansante

Ricciarelli

Torta

Vino

Aqua

Vinsanto

Grappa

Espresso

1 vineyard owner

3 fulltime workers

5 local firemen

2 guys from Elba

4 students

3 cooks

1 photographer

1 writer

2 hours

PLATE 64

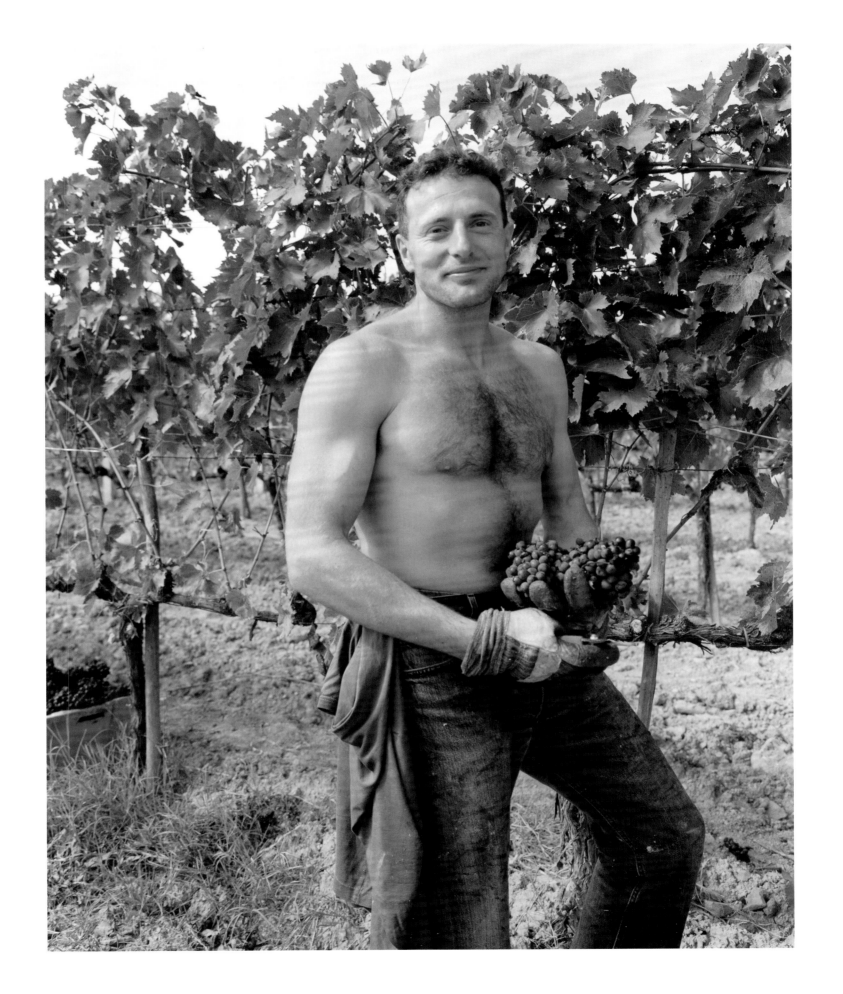

PLATE 65

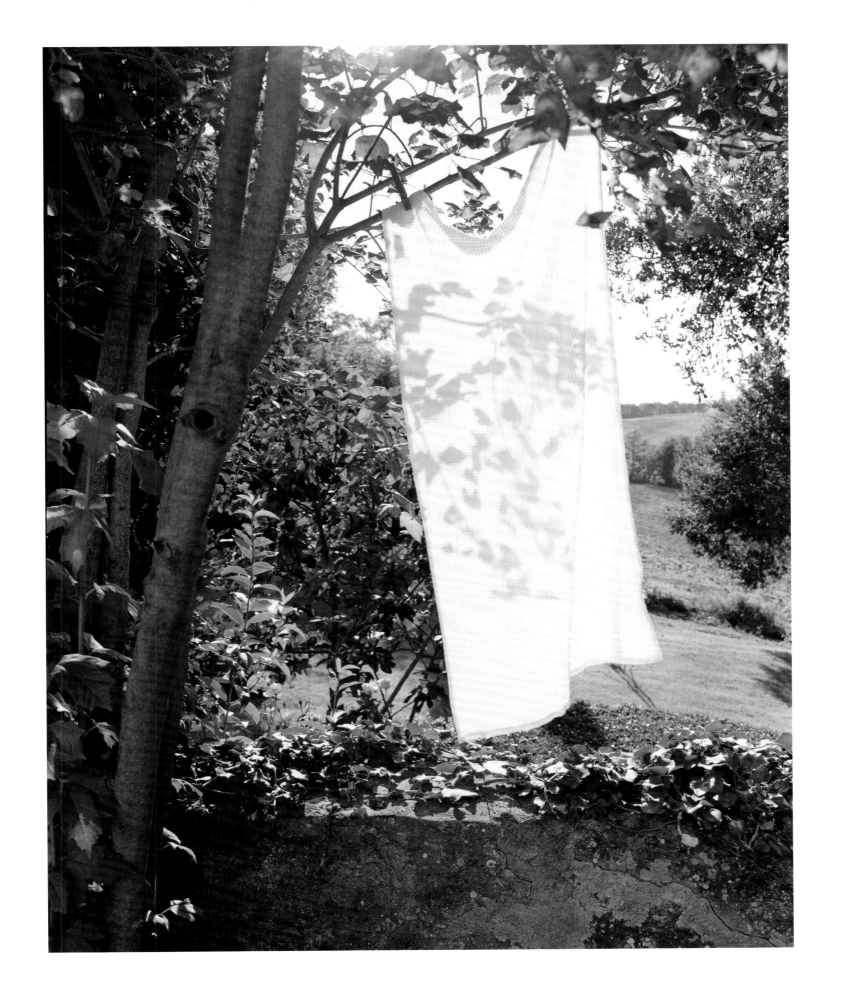

*T*he evening is still. It is every evening that ever was. Then, a sudden shiver stirs the poplars and the air is filled with dust, lit orange by the setting sun. A stair to nowhere anymore prompts a flight of the imagination. Who trod those worn steps, trailing a hand on the warmth of the iron railing? Where did they go when they turned right at the top and disappeared into an opening in the maroon ivy? A sound comes across the courtyard: a boy sings his solitary syllable for us and in this sound all language is condensed. This vowel-laden sound is his yes, his no, his come and go. His *babbo* calls to him, over and over, each syllable of the name as measured as the child's one note.

PLATE 66

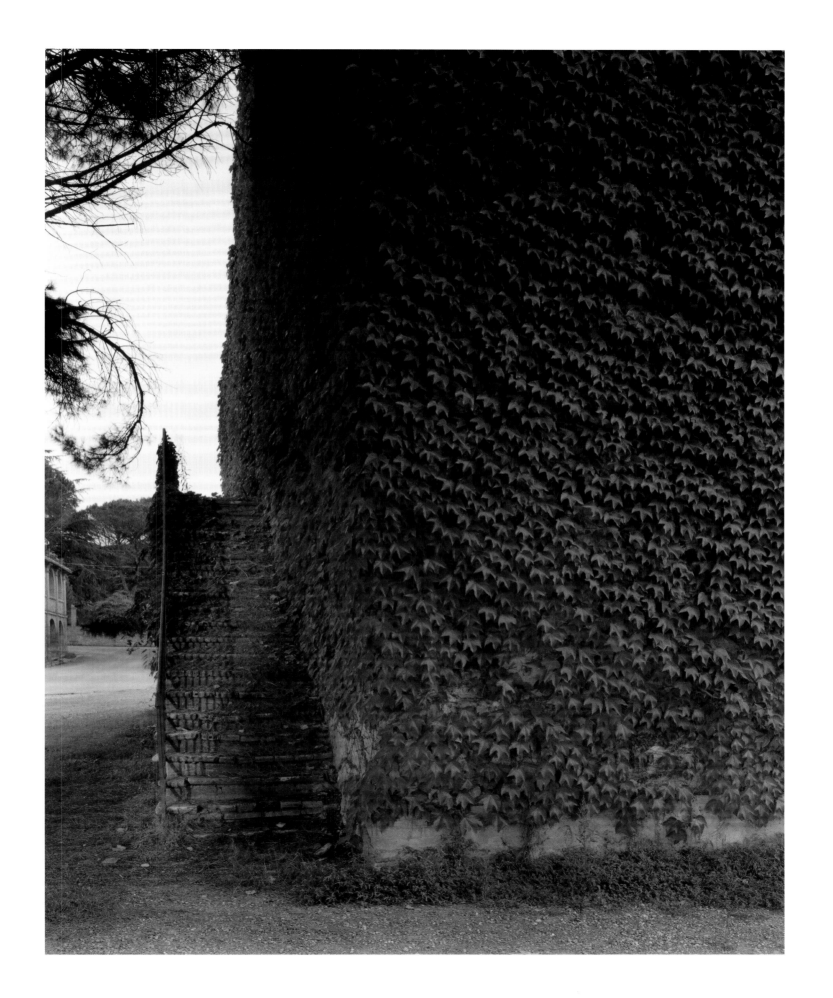

Plate 67

Overleaf: Plates 68 and 69

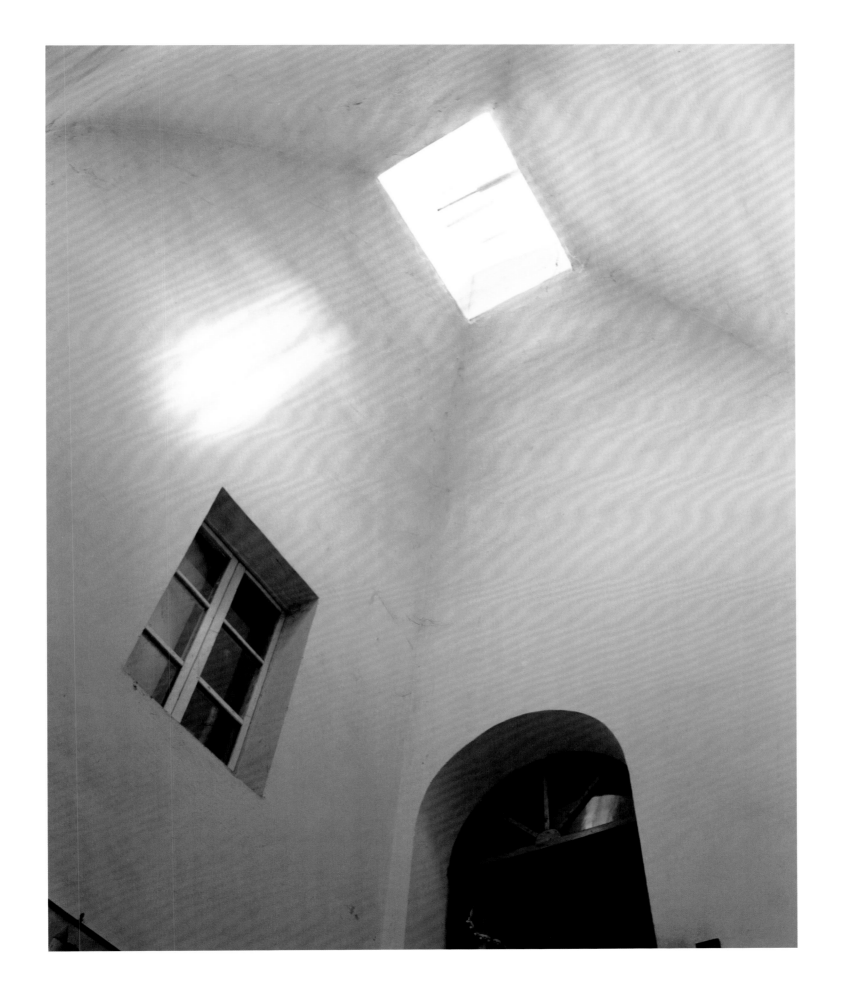

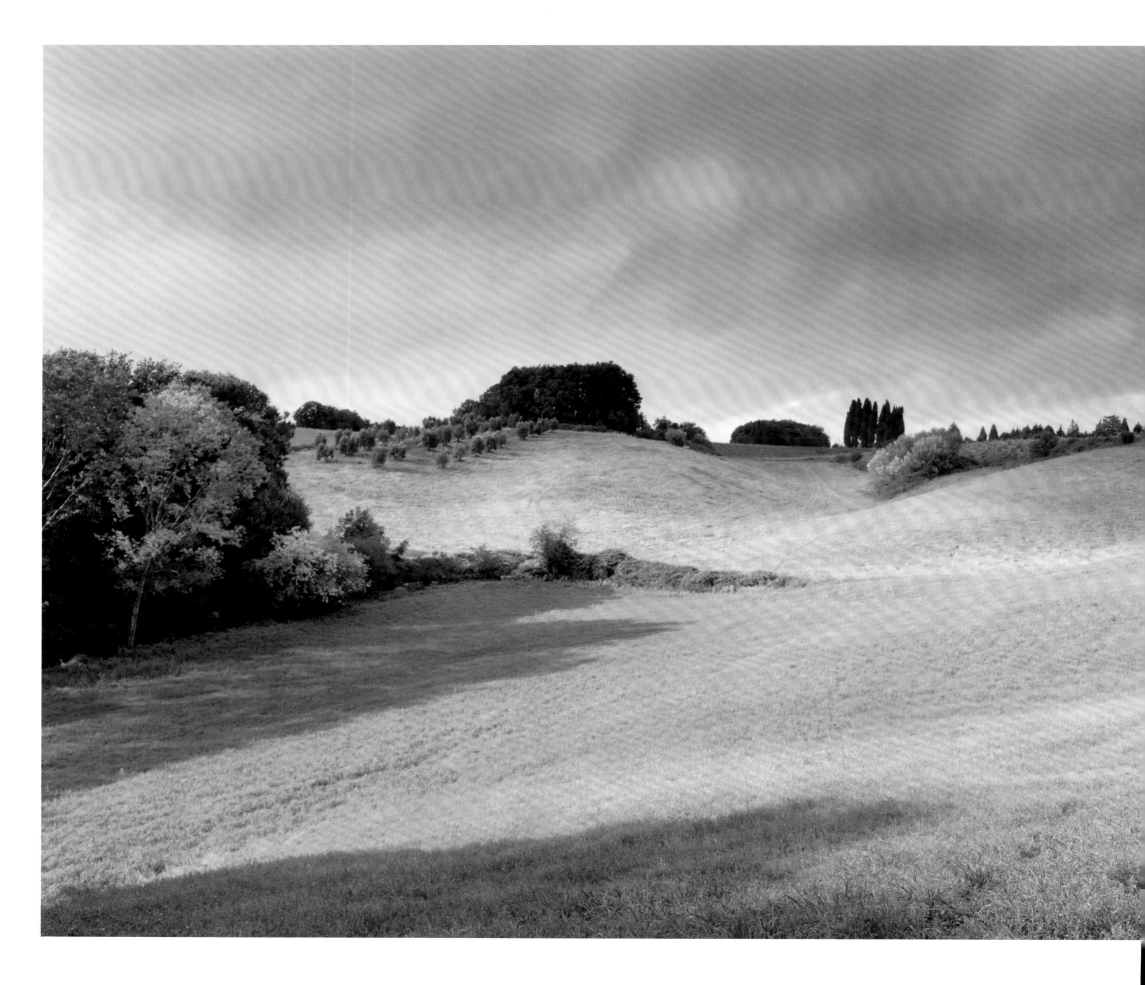

I love olive groves. There is one on the right, just before we turn off for home. I've seen it for years, but for the last two weeks it's been speaking to me like never before and I'm not sure why. I know that what pleases me visually is that the field in which the grove stands has been mown recently, leaving stripes of longer grass uniting each tree. Is that what satisfies me, this linking of the individual to the whole? Strange that in this tying together, the solitary becomes more noticeable. As the light disappears, these lines of long grass take on the same value as the trees, so that the mown field is now a faint green sea upon which each tree sails its own cresting wave. Is this the mystery that has spoken to me? The mystery of the long-gone sea, once again made present? And is this what I love so much about this land—that everywhere, all the time, there is physical and visual evidence of the accumulation of history? And is this not reassuring? For if a grove of olive trees standing in a mown field can give one thousands of years of history, then perhaps each of us, too, makes a mark by our very existence.

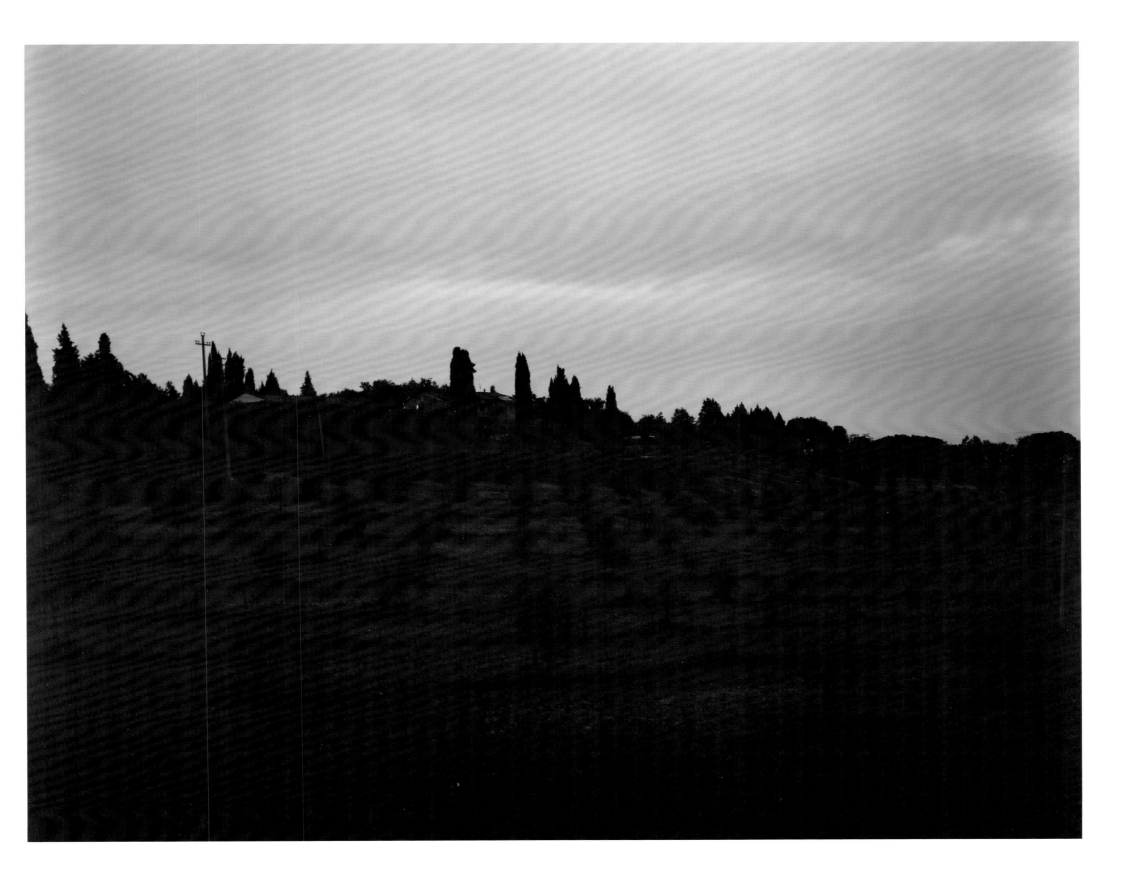

PLATE 71

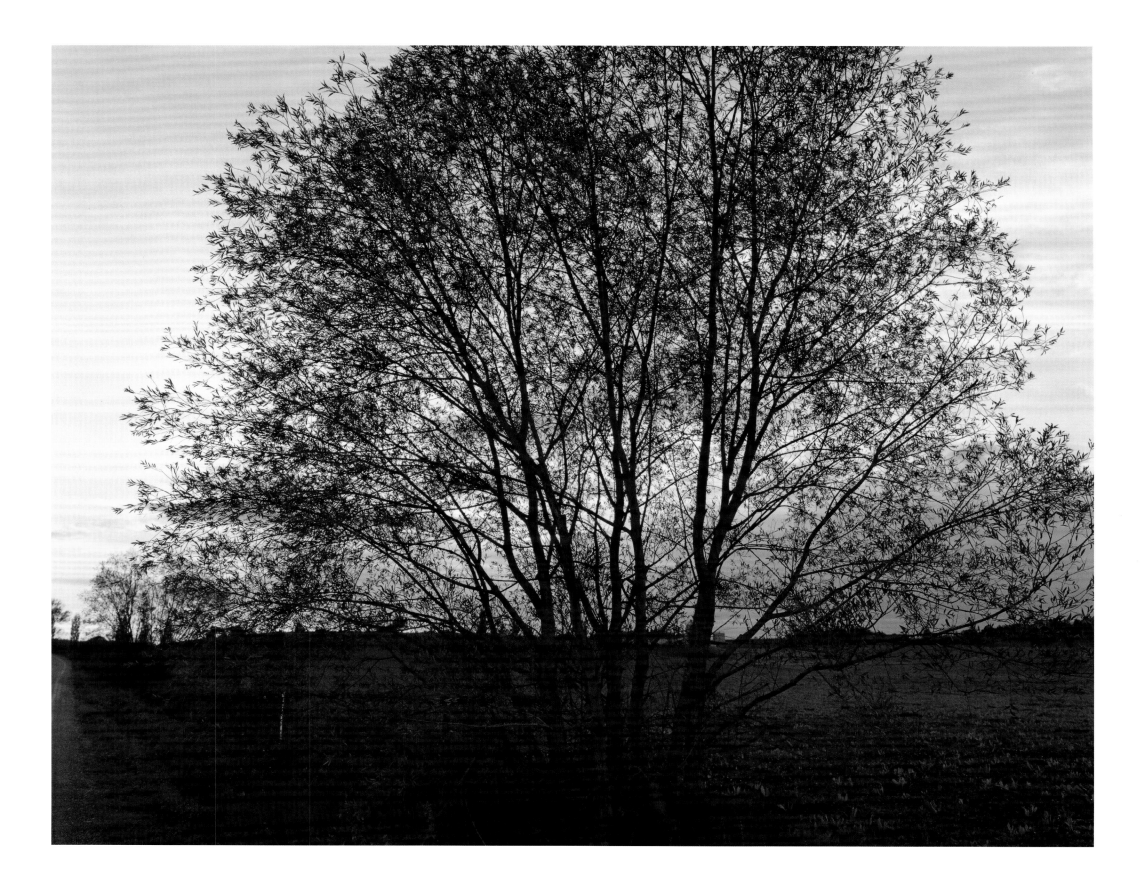

PLATE 72

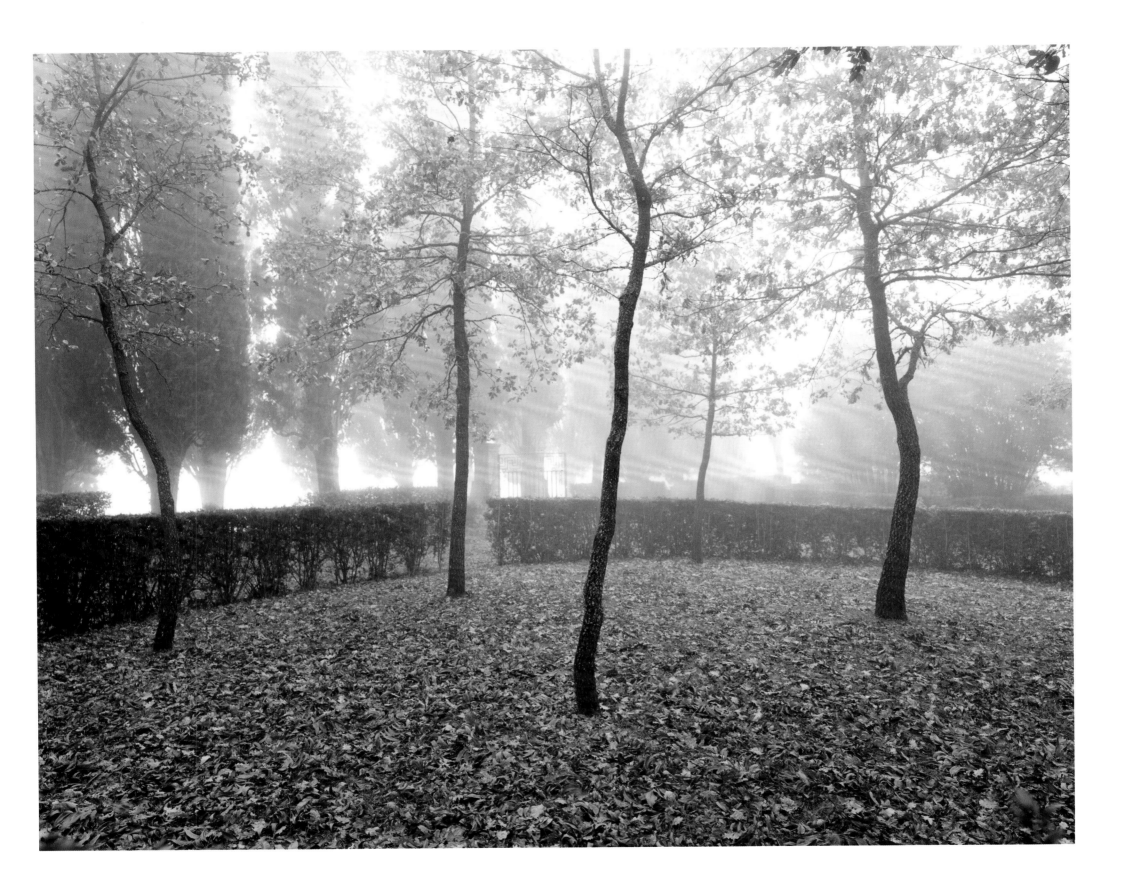

PLATE 73

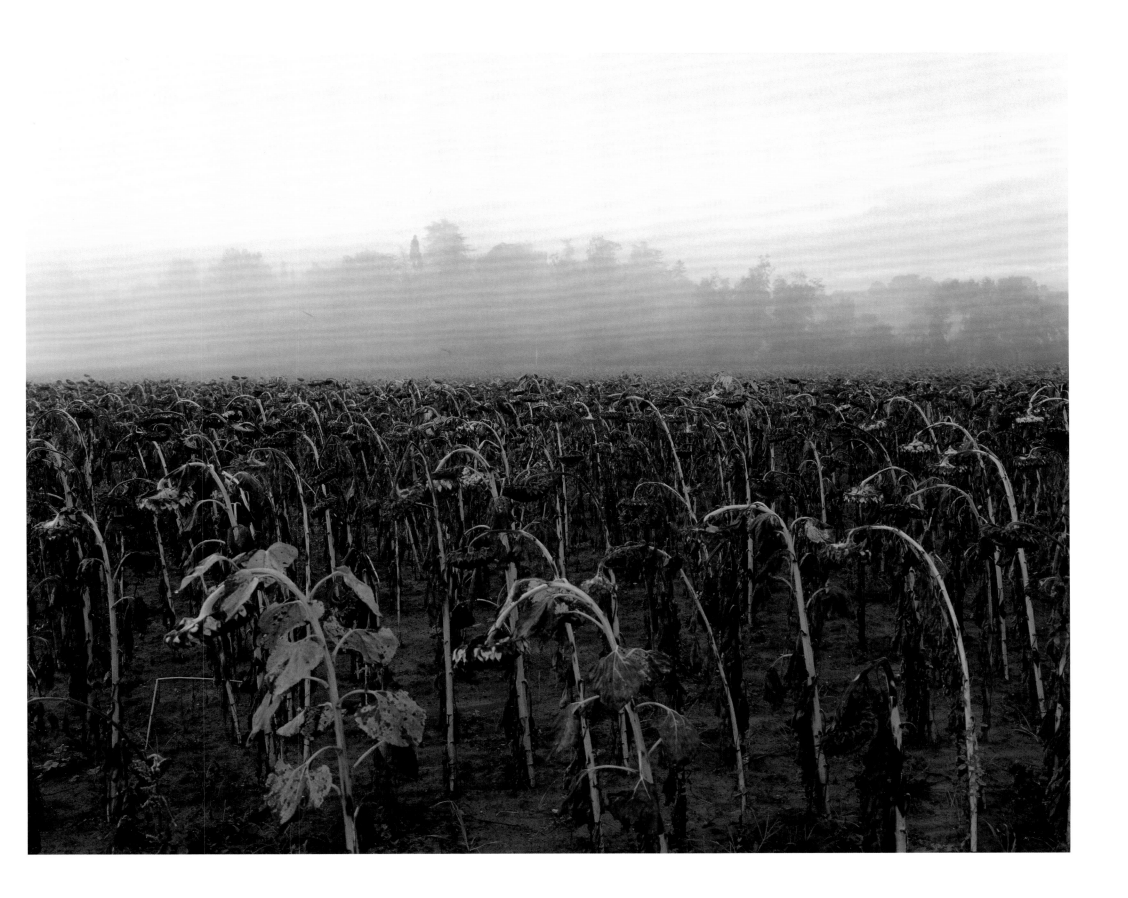

Plate 74

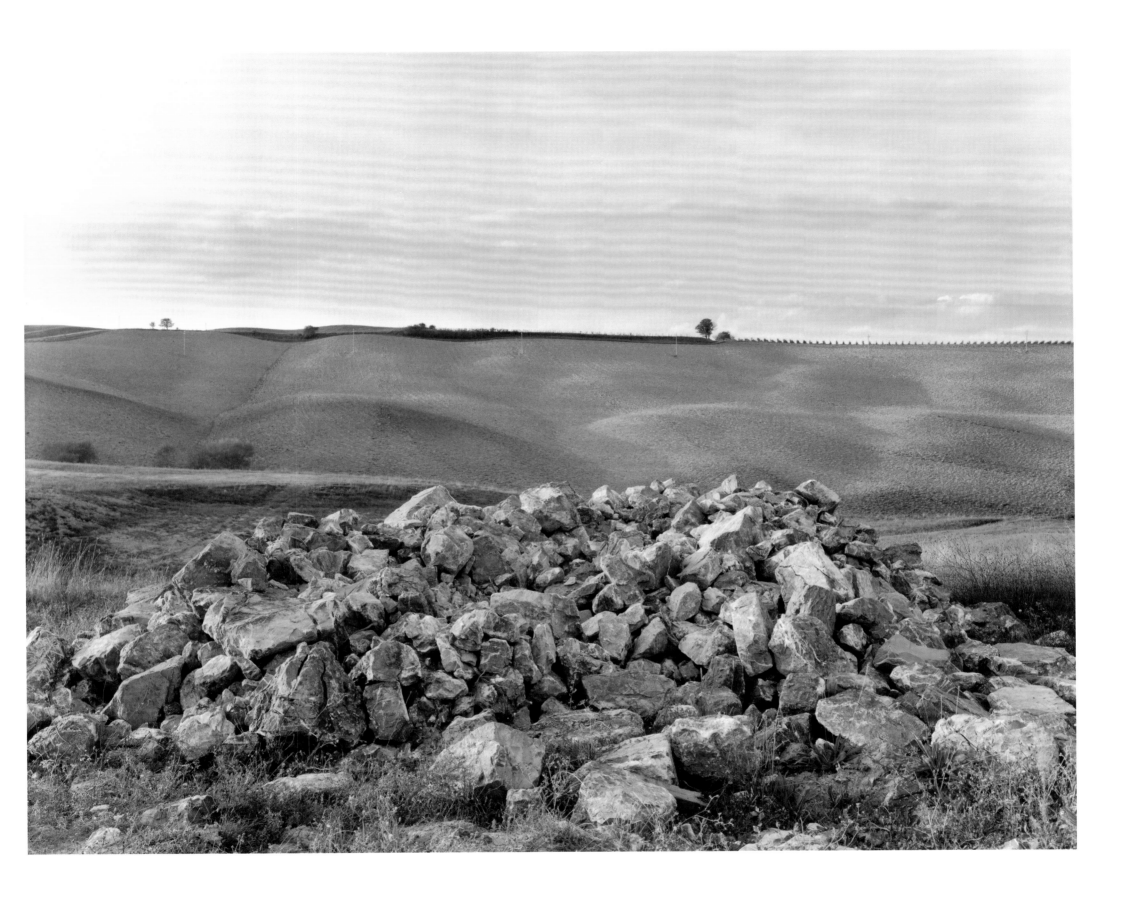

PLATE 75

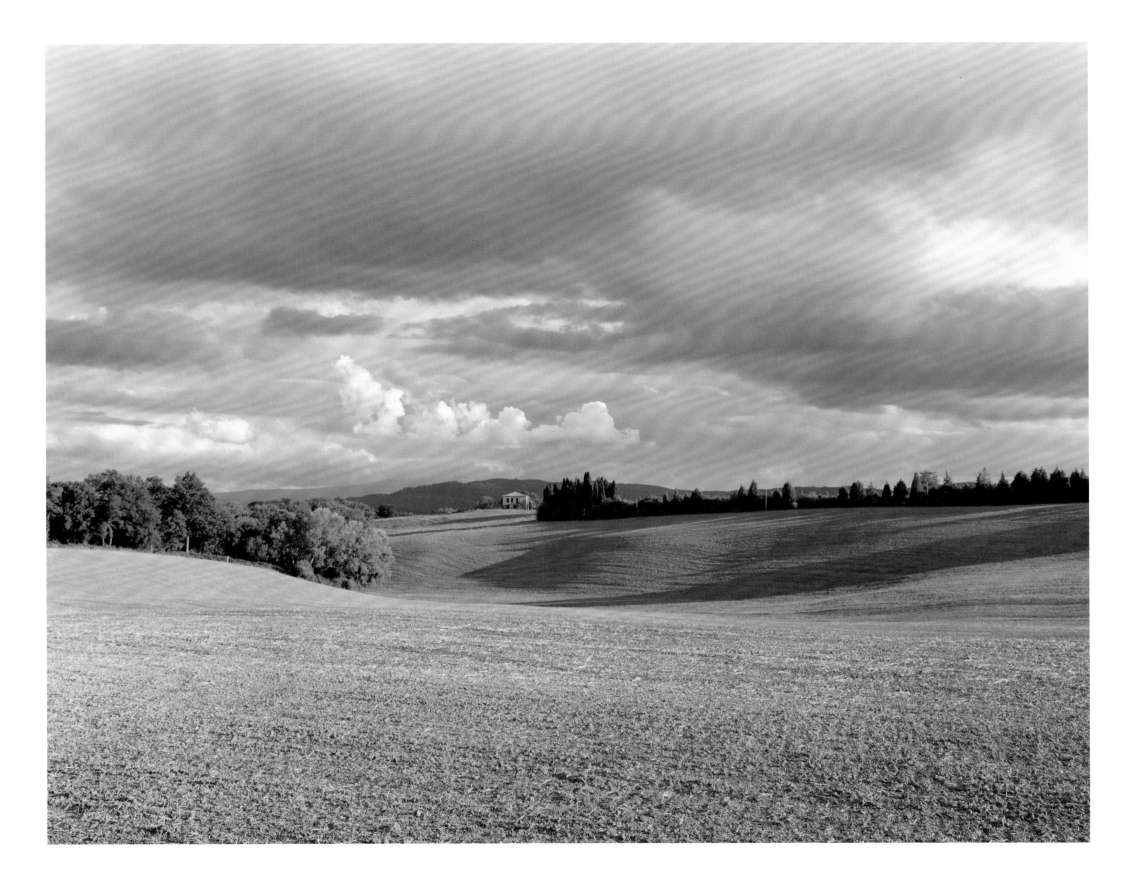

*W*e make portraits of our friends, a harvest of love. Today it is Mario and Elvio. These men are of the earth. Take the time to discuss with them the light, the shape of a hill in the morning, or the way that field is a different color in the spring, ask them the name of any plant or tree, remark on the beauty of the day or the serenity of the evening, and they will turn to you with smiles and tell you everything you have experienced…and more. The truth is we only visit this land, they live it. We are fortunate, they are blessed. So we stand now, in the last season, by a vast field of tilled earth and expect, any moment, to see it move forward and undulate at our feet. This sea of pale, dry sod holds in its emptiness the possibility of all that is to come. And what will be next? Wheat, potatoes, sunflowers, corn? Like the spokes of a wheel, these rotating crops keep the engine of cultivation rolling. Long may it come and go. Long may our friends live here and pass on their knowledge and wisdom, their tradition and spirit, and long may we be allowed to bow before it, to look and breathe it in and germinate it. For good land and its traditions are more important to the world than ever before.

PLATE 76

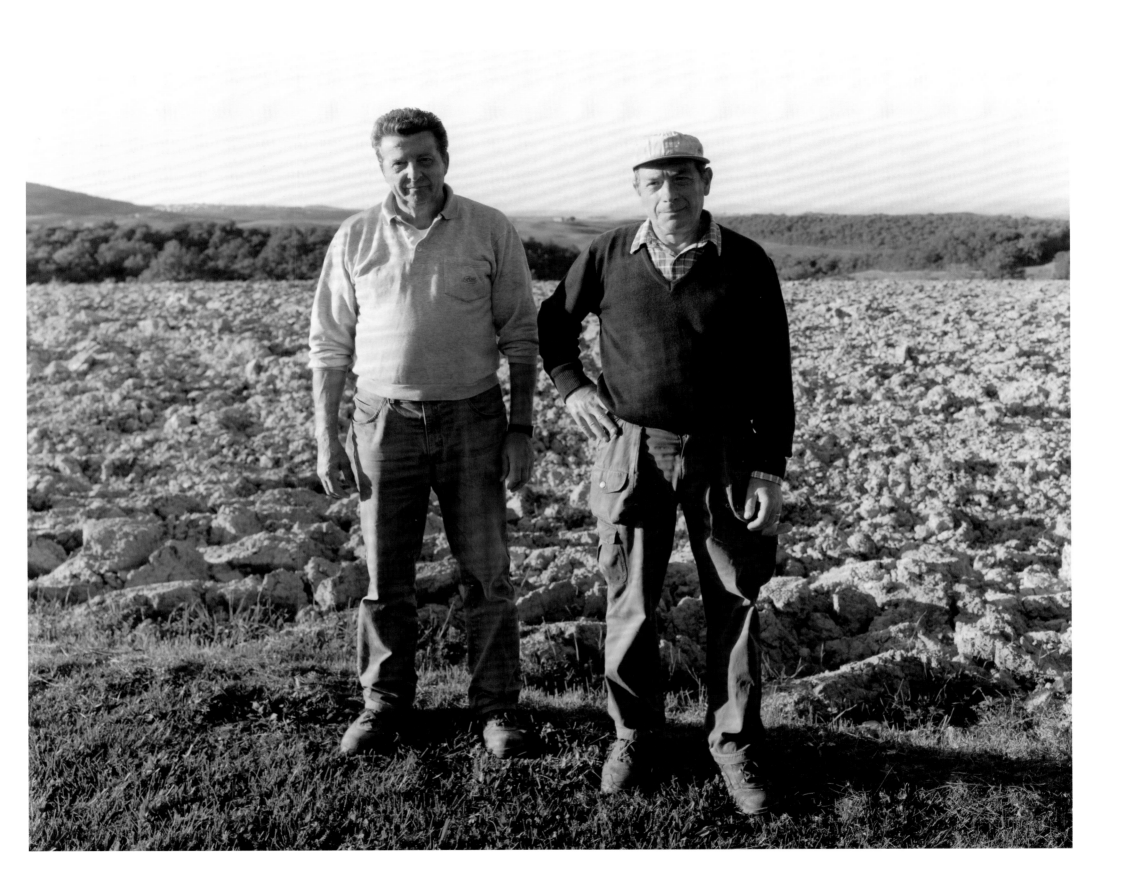

*G*ianni asks me am I taking notes for the photograph?

Am I explaining what the camera sees? I tell him the photographs need no explanation. This is a book

of marriage: between two people, two mediums, two visions. So when we sit in Gianni's house and

look, really look, we see that the house represents a way of life that most of us have turned from.

A way of life that is about having only what you need, when you need it. And those needs are directly

linked to the land. It's all about food—the one thing we all still need. Here are the tools: scythes, saws,

tongs, clippers, axes, hammers, knives, presses, scales, and sieves, handmade, to tend the land, to grow

the food, to harvest the crops, to press the grapes, to butcher the meat. Here are the tools to thresh

the hemp, to make the string, to weave the baskets. Here is the hearth to bake the bread and warm

the soup. This house is the essence of Gianni, and for us, Gianni is the essence of Toscana. For in the

end, while the land may feed our eyes and our bellies, it is our relationships that feed our hearts.

We came here because of the light, because the light is an intrinsic part of the life here and because

people like Gianni and his family keep the light burning for us all.

PLATE 77

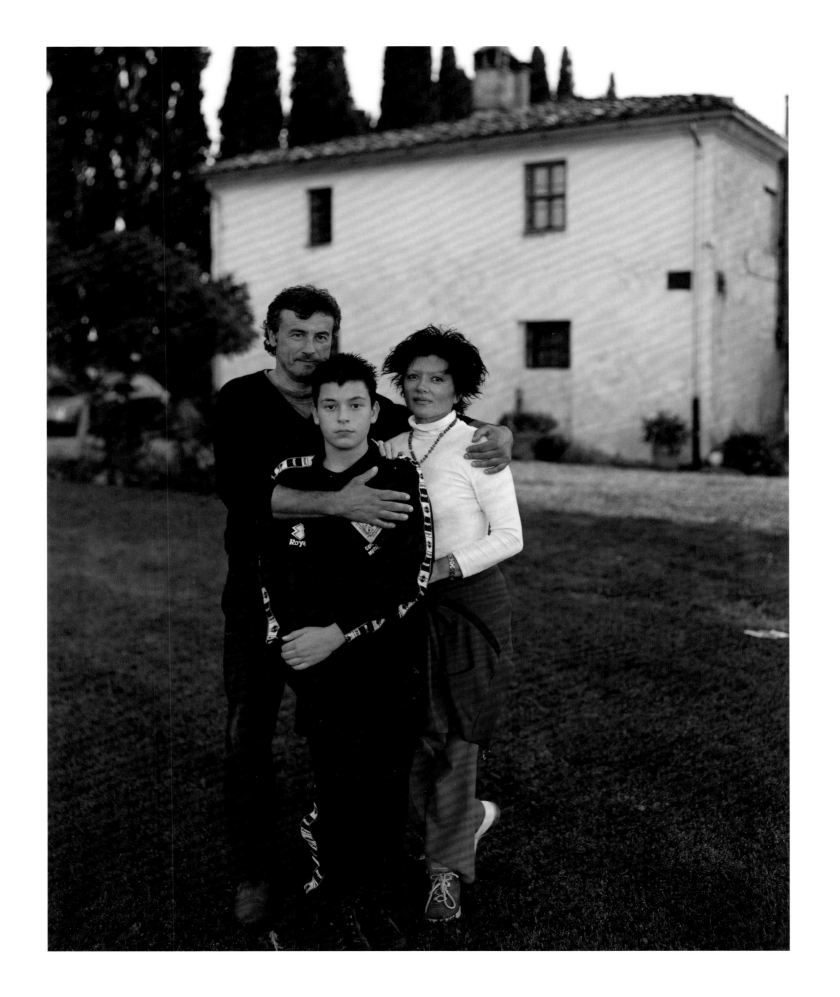

PLATE 78

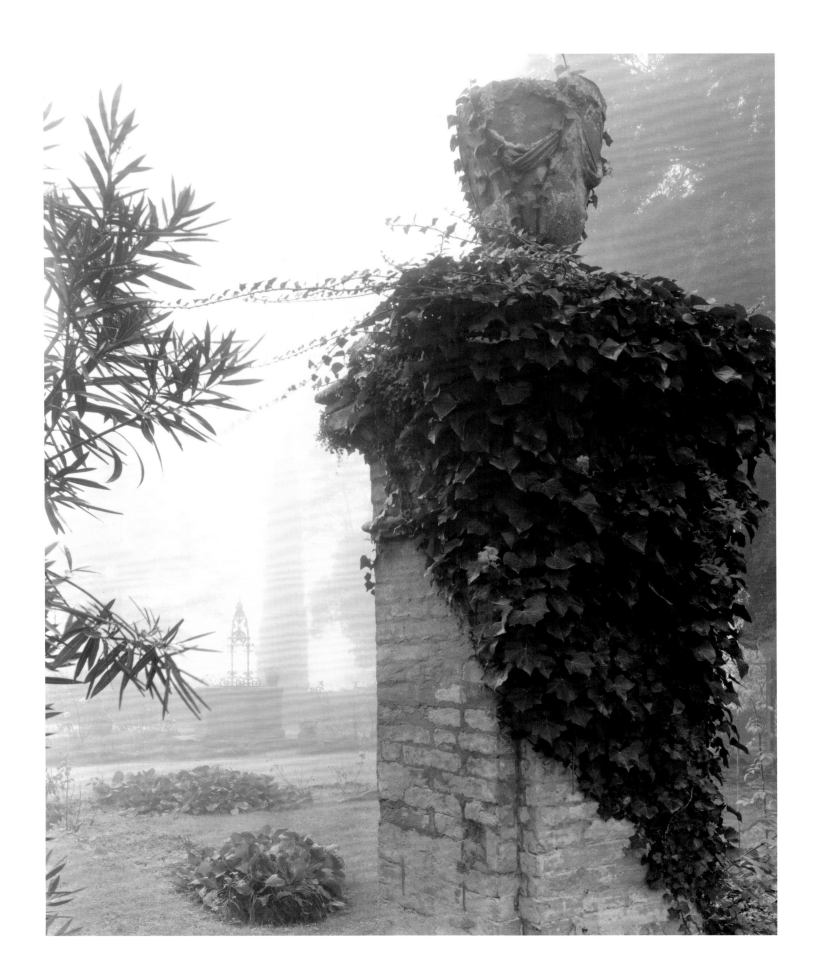

PLATE 79

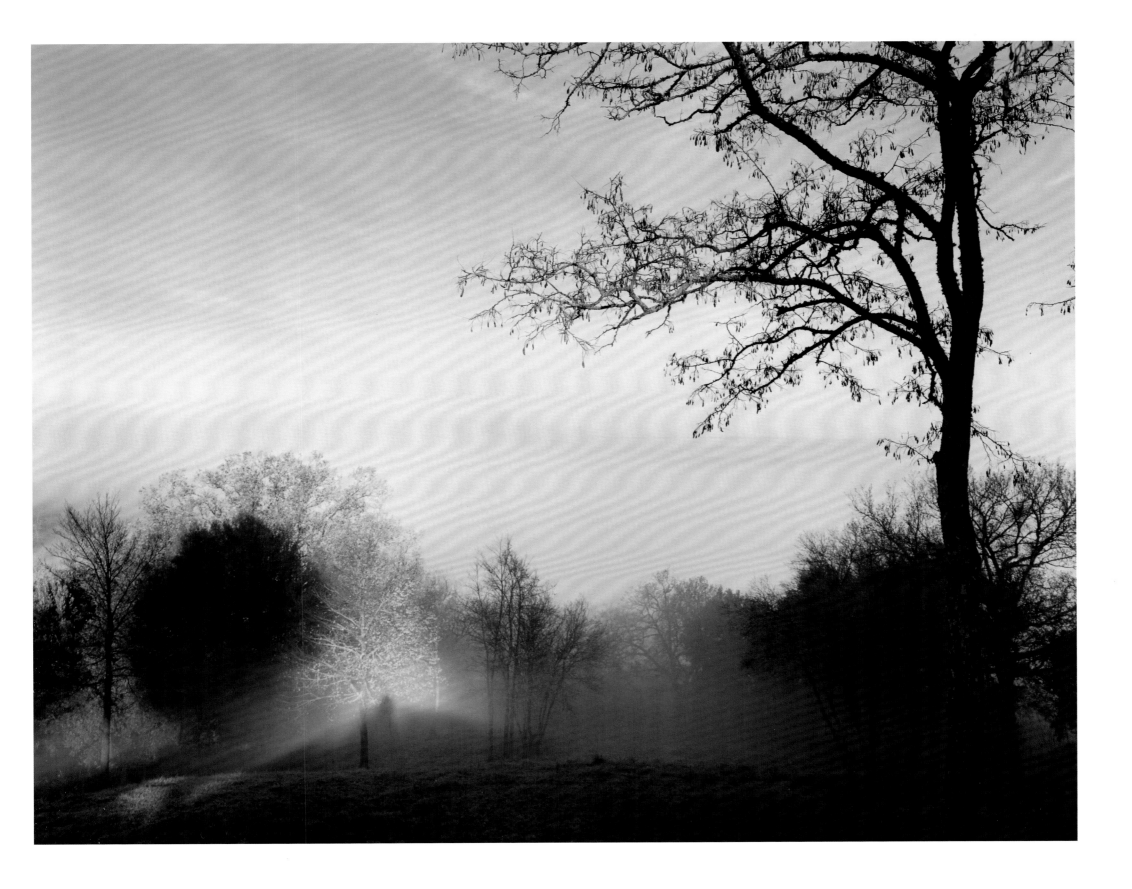

LIST OF PLATES

Overture 1: Winter—Late Afternoon
Overture 2: Spring—Vineyard, Passing Storm
Overture 3: Summer—Early Morning Mist, Rising
Overture 4: Autumn—Last Light

WINTER

Plate 1	Trees in Mist
Plate 2	Cypresses, Early Morning
Plate 3	Landscape, Midmorning
Plate 4	Rolling Hills and Cloud
Plate 5	Red Field, Dusk
Plate 6	Hill with New Grass
Plate 7	Rumpled Field
Plate 8	Frost on Turned Field
Plate 9	The River, Late Afternoon
Plate 10	Castle Woods in Mist
Plate 11	Two Trees
Plate 12	Two Columns
Plate 13	Ivy Wall
Plate 14	Olive Grove
Plate 15	The Woodcutter's Art
Plate 16	Winter Ritual
Plate 17	The Dinner Table
Plate 18	Young Trees in Winter
Plate 19	The Mist Has Frozen
Plate 20	The Land, Dusk
Plate 21	Wisteria

SPRING

Plate 22	Wisteria in Bloom
Plate 23	The Gate
Plate 24	The Chapel
Plate 25	The Day the Air Turned Green
Plate 26	Dining Room Table
Plate 27	Confessional
Plate 28	Crypt, Relic
Plate 29	The Fireplace
Plate 30	Cypresses, Moonrise
Plate 31	Tree and Stick
Plate 32	Spring Is Eternal
Plate 33	First Bloom
Plate 34	Young Trees in Spring
Plate 35	Fields in Spring (Left)
Plate 36	(Center)
Plate 37	(Right)
Plate 38	Field of Poppies
Plate 39	Storm in the Valley (Left)
Plate 40	(Right)
Plate 41	Road in Springtime
Plate 42	Grass in Olive Grove

SUMMER

Plate 43   Wheat Field, Late Afternoon
Plate 44   Olive Trees
Plate 45   Road in Summer
Plate 46   Hayfields
Plate 47   Young Girl
Plate 48   Life on the Street
Plate 49   White Road
Plate 50   Chapel in Morning Mist
Plate 51   Interior
Plate 52   The Well, Late Afternoon
Plate 53   Arches
Plate 54   Maggie and Cypress Tree
Plate 55   Road to the Sea
Plate 56   Sea and Sky
Plate 57   Summer Evening, After Storm

AUTUMN

Plate 58   Peppo
Plate 59   A September Day
Plate 60   The Linden Tree
Plate 61   Hill and Pine in Mist
Plate 62   The Gift
Plate 63   Harvesting the Grapes
Plate 64   Man with Grapes
Plate 65   Towel Drying in the Sun
Plate 66   Last Light
Plate 67   Interior, Stairwell
Plate 68   Vineyard, Late Afternoon (Left)
Plate 69   (Right)
Plate 70   Nightfall
Plate 71   Clouds and Tree, Dusk
Plate 72   Circle of Trees
Plate 73   Waiting for the Harvest
Plate 74   Fields and Stones, Late Afternoon
Plate 75   Fields and House
Plate 76   Mario and Elvio
Plate 77   Gianni, Luanna, Giovanni
Plate 78   Courtyard, Early Morning
Plate 79   First Light

STERLING and the distinctive Sterling logo are registered trademarks of Sterling Publishing Co., Inc.

2   4   6   8   10   9   7   5   3

Published by Sterling Publishing Co., Inc.
387 Park Avenue South, New York, NY 10016

Photography © 2003 by Joel Meyerowitz
Text © 2003 by Maggie Barrett

Distributed in Canada by Sterling Publishing
C/o Canadian Manda Group, 165 Dufferin Street
Toronto, Ontario, Canada M6K 3H6
Distributed in the United Kingdom by GMC Distribution Services
Castle Place, 166 High Street, Lewes, East Sussex, England BN7 1XU
Distributed in Australia by Capricorn Link (Australia) Pty. Ltd.
P.O. Box 704, Windsor, NSW 2756, Australia

Printed in China
All rights reserved

Sterling ISBN 978-1-4027-7997-8

For information about custom editions, special sales, premium and
corporate purchases, please contact Sterling Special Sales
Department at 800-805-5489 or specialsales@sterlingpublishing.com.

ACKNOWLEDGMENTS

*L*ike all successful marriages, this one—between image and text—owes much to the many people who believed in it and lent their support.

First among these is Gianni Mariotti, without whose help, friendship, and deep knowledge of all things Tuscan our work would have been more work than the pure joy it was. And thanks go to the Venturini family on whose estate we made our home over the four seasons it took to complete our book. The work of processing and printing done by Scott Hagendorf of LTI Labs in New York and Bob Korn Imaging on Cape Cod required exquisite control and was consistently of the highest quality. We particularly want to thank Jorge Ochoa and Philip Heying for making the master prints with Joel and never ceasing to work toward the most subtle and luminous rendering of the images. So, too, photographs are only as good as the film they're made on, and for that we have to thank Kodak for generously supporting this project. Our heartfelt thanks and gratitude to Joel's studio staff, without whose hard work and loyalty this book could never have been made. They are: Ember Rilleau, Susan Jenkins, John Saponara, Jon Smith, Liz Jonckheer, Ali Silverstein, Lauren Knighton, Lisa Mauceri, Melissa Piechucki, and Carre Bevilacqua. Getting around in Tuscany was made easier by the generous support of Auto Europe car rental of Maine. To all our Tuscan friends who took us into their homes and hearts we are forever grateful. Their spirit is with us every day and renews our faith in the inherent goodness of humanity.

We must, of course, thank the many people at Barnes & Noble whose belief and support in our project brought it to the elegant finish we see here. Every one of them showed an integrity that made this publishing experience a thrill. They are: Jeff Batzli, for his exquisite design; Michael Fragnito, for his guidance; Susan Lauzau, whose light touch and insight as an editor are deeply appreciated; Karen Greenberg and Michael Vagnetti, for shepherding the book so caringly through production; and Lee Stern, for his enthusiastic support.

And most of all, our everlasting gratitude and thanks to Michael Friedman and Chris Bain who, by asking us to collaborate on this book, gave us the best wedding present imaginable.

A NOTE ON THE FINE ART PRINT

The vellum envelope at the back of *Tuscany* contains a fine art print of *Castle Woods in Mist*, one of Joel Meyerowitz's most popular photographs of Tuscany. The enclosed print is reproduced on 200 gsm Garda Pat 13 Kiara paper, and is printed stochastically by 1010 Printing International Ltd., in China.

Castle Woods in Mist is also reproduced on Plate 10 of this book, in the Winter chapter.

A NOTE ON THE PRODUCTION

Tuscany is composed largely in the font known as Gill Sans, designed by noted British sculptor, graphic artist, and type designer Eric Gill in 1928–32. It is one of the most recognizable sans serif fonts in the world, still used widely today. Additional fonts used are Mrs. Eaves, a revival of the classic Baskerville font, designed by Zuzana Licko in 1996; Charme, designed in 1958 by Helmut Matheis; Ovidius, designed by Thaddeus Szumilas in 2001; Goudy, designed by Frederic W. Goudy in 1915; and Torino Modern, designed by Bob Alonso in 2000. The cover features Requiem, an old-style serif typeface designed by Jonathan Hoefler in 1992.

Tuscany is printed on 170 gsm matte art paper, and bound in T-Saifu cloth.

Printed and bound by 1010 Printing International Ltd., in China.